Amazon revie

'An excellent and intriguing plot, very well written. The author's storytelling is creative and the narrative flows well. I gobbled this book up!'

'I'm loving this book and it is making me laugh out loud. The characters are convincing and the plot flows beautifully.'

'Feelgood, warm and cosy, the perfect antidote to the times we live in.'

'The gentle pace of the unfolding story had me in its grip from the outset. I will look for more books by Susanna Scott.'

'All the characters are mixed and fun, it made me smile a lot. Altogether a happy read.'

'This is the second book from this author and she didn't disappoint. I do hope there is a book 3!'

'Well written, it draws you in. I couldn't put it down.'

Susanna Scott lives in a seaside town on the Yorkshire Coast. She loves her family, gardening, nature, reading and writing books. The last was discovered during the first lockdown when it gave her time and peace to 'have a go' at something she has wanted to do since she was a child. She loves being out in the Yorkshire countryside, be it Dales, Moors or the Coast and finds inspiration for her writing there. She is NOT employed by the Yorkshire tourist board – honest!

Also by Susanna Scott

The Gypsy Caravan
The Winterfell Stone

(and for children)
Robin Hood and the Wolfshead Tree.

Susanna Scott @yorkshirecoastwriter on Facebook
and
Susanna Scott author page on Amazon

WEAVER'S GREEN

Susanna Scott

To Lisa, Jamie and Ben with thanks for your love
and encouragement.

Chapter 1

As her destination loomed ever nearer, Tess remembered the fateful conversation with her father that had set her on this course and had sealed her doom. Well, for a couple of weeks at least.

'But she's always been crazy!' she had whined to him, reverting to the teenage girl she had been when she last saw her great-aunt and not the supposedly sensible, if aimless and jobless, woman of nearly thirty she was now.

'Tess, I didn't say she was crazy. I said she was going through a bad patch and not making a lot of sense. Understandable after she found her brother's dead body like that. It must have been terrible for her.'

Tess's father had always been the Black Sheep of the family. After deviating from their family's usual way of life, he had embarked on a shocking career move which had ended up with him here. The rectory of St. Mary's in the Field church in Norfolk where he was The Reverend Eustace d'Evreux.

Of course, the pagan beliefs of the other branch of the d'Evreux family were not paraded above the surface but bubbled there below in a seething mass of rumour and hearsay.

Personally, she blamed Great Aunt Elspeth for the embarrassment that was her name, not something that should ever be inflicted on a shy teenager. She had been in her last year at school when her father had dragged her over to the remote moorland village, lurking in a valley on the North Yorkshire Moors. He was intent on building bridges, with Tess as the sacrificial lamb. He had managed it to an extent, visiting her yearly ever since. Thankfully without Tess. Her younger brother Francis lived and worked in Paris so he got out of it nicely too.

As teenagers do, she had sat there in silence, shrugging occasionally. She had lost her mother when she was nine years old and had withdrawn into herself afterwards anyway, without being subjected to this woman. The only time she

8

spoke, she wished she'd kept quiet as it put her off her great aunt for life. She had suffered her schooldays under the name of d'Evreux. 'Ooh – posh!' or 'Huh, French are you?' and 'Don't think you're better than me just because I'm called Jones!' Tess wished she had been called Jones.

Tess mentioned this wish after a discussion between her father and great-aunt on the family name and how respected it was. Elspeth had pulled herself up to her full Valkyrie height of six feet and thundered,

'It is a Noble Name! WE CAME OVER WITH THE CONQUEROR!'

That was the last time Tess could be persuaded to visit, as she fervently wished that The Conqueror had left Gaspard d'Evreux living happily on his farm or wherever and not brought him to start the English side of the family. She did realise that the English d'Evreux included her and she might never have been born otherwise but she didn't allow reason to interfere with indignation.

She had come away with the firm impression that her great aunt was a witch, the black cat in the kitchen was her familiar and Satan dwelt within those walls.

Now, nearly twelve years later, she drove along the coastal road towards Whitby. On either side of her were wide open spaces of moorland, the heather just beginning to show the brightly-coloured flowers which transformed it into a sea of purple every summer.

She was in the middle of nowhere and could see no markers as to where she was. She had passed a huge valley further back in which a steam train was quaintly puffing along the valley bottom and apart from an unused Inn, boarded up and looking sorry for itself, she might as well have been on an alien, uninhabited planet.

After another mile, she saw a signpost and a narrow single track, turning off for the ancient village of Weaver's Green. Her destination..

Tess was yet another mile down the lane and still couldn't see any signs of a village. She knew it was hidden in a valley somewhere. She drove over a cattle grid and narrowly avoided various sheep trying to attach themselves to the front bumper of the car as they meandered across the lane. After a while, she came to the conclusion that Weaver's Green was the Yorkshire equivalent of Brigadoon and hid itself from sight for a hundred years.

Suddenly, as she crested a ridge, the sun came out and lit the moors for miles around, showing every cleft and shallow, hill and valley ahead of her. There, settled comfortably in the bottom of a large moorland basin was Weaver's Green. It didn't look anywhere as near as forbidding as she remembered it but then the sun always put a different complexion on things.

Tess pulled her car over onto a smooth, grassy plateau to her left and got out, unfolding her slim. gamine body from the cramped confines of her Mini Clubman. Looking around her, she saw a large white boulder, which would be perfect to sit on and have her late lunch. She had kept driving as, if she'd stopped, she might have turned the car back towards Norfolk. While she ate it she could steel herself for the forthcoming meeting with Great Aunt Elspeth – the eldest now, of the d'Evreux family that CAME OVER WITH THE CONQUEROR!

Turning back with her egg mayonnaise sandwiches and flask of coffee, she searched in vain for the white boulder which seemed to have disappeared. She did, however, see a large white sheep ambling off with a disgruntled 'Baa-aa', possibly not wanting to be used as a seat. They're everywhere, thought Tess, they all wandered around pretending to be something else.

She found another patch of grass which all the sheep had munched to a smooth, moss-like texture and sat down to eat. While she finished off her coffee, she contemplated the village further down the hill, of which she realised she had little memory, instead focussing on her Great Aunt's house and the lack of welcome therein.

There were quite a few houses but they were spread along the sides of the country lanes criss-crossing through it. By far the biggest concentration of houses was around the green, a little further on from the old Norman church. She vaguely remembered a few shops standing on one side while the houses spread out on the others. It looked rather pleasant, she had to admit but it really didn't help. She really wasn't looking forward to this encounter at all. With a bit of luck, Elspeth would send her straight back. Although – and here Tess sighed because she had a kind heart underneath her occasionally ungracious manner – if Elspeth really was depressed, and she could help in any way, then she would.

Her father said his aunt had sounded strange on the phone and said she was missing his presence very much, even though it was well known that she couldn't stand her eldest brother and they rarely talked as the feeling was mutual. 'Howling at the Moon' was also mentioned in a stream of consciousness that Eustace had found hard to decipher. A mysterious nephew had turned up to claim his uncle's estate too and although this was in Hugo's will, Elspeth seemed to have taken an active dislike to the man. So all in all, Tess supposed her father had a point. Maybe she did need help. Tess had been made redundant after over eight years in a job she hated so she had no excuse anyway, as she was just cluttering up the vicarage.

Great Uncle Hugo d'Evreux had no children but Eustace had recalled stories of his wife of less than two years, having a sister, so it could be all above board and would fit in with the enmity between sister and eldest brother. There was one thing for sure – apart from Elspeth, who had apparently been left some money but not the house, there was only the Reverend Eustace d'Evreux and his daughter left to leave anything to. Hugo would rather leave his estate to the Netherley Bottom Village Society of Satanists than leave a penny to a god-fearing black sheep of the family who dared to conform to normality. He had never spoken to Eustace and had ignored his younger brother, Tess's grandfather William too. They had fallen out before William had died, which was before Tess was born so she never knew him. Tess sighed. The d'Evreux family. If their family history was in book form, it would have been written by Bram Stoker and then adapted for film by Hammer Horror.

Chapter 2

As Tess drove into the village, she slowed down near to her great aunt's house, the second house she came to, and then set off again to the village green a little further on. She wasn't quite ready for the confrontation yet, although she knew she was only putting off the inevitable. She would look in the shops and perhaps take a little peace offering as she had an idea that her visit to Wykeham Grange would be as welcome to Elspeth as it was to herself.

Parking next to the green, she was on her way to the shops when she saw a large, brightly coloured barrow over by a row of cottages at the far side of the green. Approaching it, she saw that the colour came from a variety of different flowers arranged in buckets. Perfect, Tess thought, I'll take the great aunt some flowers to sweeten her. No one can resist flowers.

She picked a bunch of phlox and knocked on the nearest door. It was a neat little end-of-terrace cottage with a door painted in a mossy green. Just as she heard someone start to open the door, she heard a stranger noise. It sounded like the owner of the cottage smoked sixty a day or had a nasty cough. Tess instinctively stepped back.

The door was flung open by a young woman around Tess's age. She was wearing baggy, flowered trousers with a long cheesecloth tunic and holding her long dark, curly hair back was a flowered hairband. She looked like a throwback to the hippie days. She did, however, wear a welcoming smile and didn't look in the slightest bit ill.

'Hi' she smiled, 'are those the ones you want?'

Tess held them out to her and fished in her purse for the right money.

'Shall I wrap the stems in damp newspaper for you? Have you got far to go?' asked the new-age person in front of her. She was a little on the plump side but it suited her and her face was so rosy and happy-looking.

'No, I'm visiting my great aunt, up there, just past the church.

The lady's face dropped.

'Wykeham Grange? Miss Wykeham d'Evreux? Heaven help you then – she scares the life out of me! Oh, I'm so sorry, she's your family – I shouldn't have said that.'

Discretion obviously wasn't one of her strong points. Tess had forgotten her aunt had the Wykeham attached to her already pretentious name.

'It's quite alright, she scares the life out of me too' agreed Tess and after a moment's pause, they both collapsed in giggles and the flower lady held out her hand.

'Pleased to meet you, I'm Berry.' Seeing Tess's enquiring expression, she added 'It's short for Bernadette because I didn't want to be called Bernie. There was a Bernie when I was a kid who used to go round on his bike leering at us kids and it put me off the name for life.'

Tess laughed and introduced herself. As she did so, the strange noise sounded again, Berry laughed again at Tess's expression.

'Ah, let me introduce you to Clover and Daisy'

Although Tess didn't want to catch what sounded like whooping cough from this potential earth-mother's potential children, curiosity compelled her to follow her. She led her through a small and slightly chaotic living room and a bright sunny kitchen, then through the back door into a narrow garden. Nearest the house, the flowerbeds were showing a riot of colour with the cottage garden flowers but further down, on a smallish patch of grass, stood two donkeys.

'Oh they're lovely!' remarked Tess as the donkeys came down to the makeshift fence to greet them.

'They're rescue donkeys and this garden is far too small for them. I've only had them a few weeks but I couldn't leave them in the place I found them. I will have to keep them here until I find somewhere else to keep them. I keep trying but…'

'You'd think somewhere round here, in the middle of the country, would have enough land for them wouldn't you?' frowned Tess.

'They have but unfortunately, they are almost all manicured and formally laid out gardens. The only farm round here is a few miles away over the hill that way and the land is taken up with a touring caravan site. The smaller houses like mine have tiny gardens so… here they are. They seem happy enough at the moment. They have a shelter at the bottom there. Sort of.'

Berry grimaced and Tess looked down at a dilapidated wooden shed with an open front. The roof looked solid though.

'Although, this is luxury. You should have seen where they came from.' She shuddered and they both went quiet as they stroked Clover and Daisy's muzzles.

'Well, I suppose I'd better go into the Dragon's Lair.' sighed Tess and Berry smiled in commiseration.

As Tess, walked back to her car, Berry called out,

'Call in for a cuppa, won't you? You're welcome anytime.'

Tess shouted out her thanks and thought that she would take her up on it. She would probably need a little uncomplicated friendliness before long.

*

Tess pulled her car into the spacious gravel drive and turning the ignition off, she surveyed the large imposing house in front of her. Wykeham Grange. In her mind, it had always featured as an Addams family mansion with Morticia living inside but going by the name of Elspeth. Now, however, with the sun shining on the light, honey-coloured stone it looked, dare she say it, quite pleasant. The mullioned stone windows were set into the house and the leaded glass reflected the sun's rays, giving the whole house, unbelievably, a comfortable, lived-in look. Had her memory been playing tricks on her?

She saw an old-fashioned bell-pull, pulled it with some force and stood there, bemused. When Lurch or Morticia didn't appear after the second summons, she made her way around the gravel path to the back of the house. She stopped short and looked in amazement at the view that met her. There was the country road she had travelled on. The shadows and sunlight dancing across the flourishing heather and yellow gorse. Stands of trees, which she hadn't expected, stood sentinel over the land around them and outcrops of limestone and millstone grit. She knew it was beautiful – but she just hadn't expected the outlook from her great aunt's house to be so…breath-taking. She remembered that the rain had been coming down in sheets when they had last been here. It must have coloured her whole impression of this house. This village. The moors.

Well, she thought. This chore that had been set by her father might not turn out to be so bad after all. She turned to look at the back of the house and came to the conclusion that it was a back-to-front house. This façade was infinitely better than the comparatively featureless front. There were two wings at either side with large bay windows and between them both, someone had added a large Edwardian-style conservatory. The more she stared, she thought that the Edwardian style might be completely original. It had the look of being there for over a hundred years and had settled into itself.

With a jolt, she realised that there was a figure standing in the open doorway of the conservatory and a cut-glass voice interrupted her thoughts.

'Theresa, I expect? Although that isn't your natural hair colour.'

Tess instinctively put her hand up to her neat, copper-coloured bob. It was natural in as much as it had said Natural Burnished Copper on the bottle, she thought to herself. The tall, slender, imposing figure of her great aunt advanced towards her; her thin lips were compressed even more in annoyance. Bending a little, she stared into Tess's eyes which were an unusual bright blue with a dark rim which exaggerated their appearance even more. It was the first thing people remarked on when they met her. Tess was shocked to see that Elspeth's eyes were exactly the same. A little faded with age, a few red veins threading their way across the whites but otherwise, they were both staring into mirrors. 'Hmm' said Elspeth, drawing back at last, 'you've inherited the eyes but have you inherited the sight?' and with that, Elspeth turned and marched back into the conservatory, leaving an unsettled Tess, flowers drooping with terror in her left hand, to follow her into the Dragon's Lair.

Chapter 3

As she followed the straight-backed figure walking in front of her, Tess was aware of an oppressive silence between them. Elspeth suddenly stopped outside a door and spun around.

'My library, which I use as a study' she barked, territorially, 'I would like to be left in peace when I'm in there.'

She pointed down a dark passage in front of her to another door at the far end.

'My sitting room. I don't want to be disturbed in there either.'

Welcome to Wykeham Grange, thought Tess.

'To the left, there is a cloakroom and the utility room is next to it. Across there,' she indicated the other side of the vast tiled hall, 'is another small study and at the back is another sitting room – both of which you can use.'

'Upstairs' the stentorian voice continued in perfect Queen's English, 'the last room on the right is your bedroom, bathroom attached. Shep isn't in tonight, it's one of her days off, so there will be no cooked dinner tonight. Just help yourself to food in the kitchen' she indicated yet another door just past the utility, 'I will take mine in my sitting room, so I will no doubt see you tomorrow'

She said this with the air of someone in a hurry and expecting the bailiffs. Then she opened the door of her study and turning, evidently expecting a response.

Tess had a mad urge to curtsey and say 'Thankee M'm, obliged I'm sure.' but instead held up the wilting flowers which now seemed to be leaning away from Elspeth in a swoon.

'I've brought you these' whimpered Tess.

Then it happened. 'The Look'. The main reason she had been terrified of her great aunt all those years ago and nothing had changed. She had fixed her with a glare that pierced Tess's skull. It went on for at least ten seconds but it seemed to Tess that she was caught in an eternal laser beam from which there was no escape. Then with a look of absolute disdain and an absence of words, Elspeth entered her cave.

Still feeling that she'd been flattened by a steam-roller, Tess eventually came round and with a determined look on her face, sought out the utility room, where she found an assortment of vases. She filled a crystal one with water and plonked the flowers in it, although she didn't give much for their chances now.

Feeling safe enough in the knowledge that she would be left alone, she chanced a peep into 'her' small study. It was definitely small but had an enormous fireplace. A battered but comfortable-looking tan leather armchair stood to one side. The walls were painted dark green and the windows and paintwork were white. It looked like the inside of a Gentleman's club, not that she'd ever been in one. It was curiously restful and with the small desk under the window overlooking the side gravel drive and a few small trees, she was actually itching to sit there and write. Maybe a letter to her father to tell him that she had survived the first hour but if he didn't hear from her ever again, to think of her fondly?

She followed the passage along and found the door to 'her' sitting room and was pleasantly surprised to find it was one of the bay-windowed rooms. Sunny and light, the walls were still painted in the dark olive green of the study but were painted white above the deep picture rails.

The fireplace was black cast-iron with a central fire cage and Victorian tiles at either side. There was an emerald green velvet, squashy sofa against one wall and in the window was a small round table with a high-backed, ornately carved side chair next to it.

There was a TV in one corner and a small bookcase with an assortment of books which looked unused. Perhaps Elspeth had been given them and they had been banished to this room, not being allowed in her private library?

Best of all – she could see that wonderful view over the moors and fells at the back of the house. The burgeoning heather shone in the sun and contrasted with the large grassy, green areas. These fell away at intervals into small deep cloughs, the slopes of which were covered on both sides with trees. A haze lingered on the horizon making the stands of trees and large stone outcrops there nothing but shadows.

She had been expecting it to be dark, forbidding and bleak, which she supposed it was in winter and on the windswept tops but here, in the Weaver's Green moorland valley, the landscape was magical. It would be pleasant to sit here and read or look out of that window as it looked like she was going to be left alone to do so.

A guilty conscience nagged at her. The result of being a clergyman's daughter, she supposed. She had been sent here to help her great aunt. She was obviously a lot older than when she last saw her, her almost black hair had turned silver and was piled on her head in a cottage-loaf style of bun. Wispy stray hairs framed her face like a halo and emphasised those ultra-blue eyes. Did anyone deserve a halo less, thought Tess, uncharitably? She didn't seem like she needed help at all but Tess knew that grief showed itself in different ways for different people.

According to her father, Elspeth missed Hugo terribly, which even he was very puzzled by. She was also imagining or hearing things. Tess felt she ought to be more compassionate. She also hoped she could dig down deep and find this compassion because, left to her own devices, all she wanted to do was high-tail it out of there.

*

Tess sat straight up in her bed and looked around. What had woken her? The next second, she knew. An unearthly howl echoed around the valley behind them. She froze and slowly turned to look at the bedside clock. She was stupidly comforted to know that it wasn't the stroke of midnight but eleven-forty pm instead Although, a howl was still a howl.

She had only been asleep for twenty minutes but was now wide awake. She went over to the window – her bedroom was above her sitting room – and put her face against it. There was nothing much to see as the moon was behind a cloud. She waited a few minutes, listening out again with her nerves taut and senses heightened but there was nothing more.

Sitting on the bed, she remembered her father had said Elspeth mentioned 'howling at the moon' but he couldn't make head nor tail of it. Maybe her great-aunt wasn't going round the bend after all. Knowing that sleep wouldn't come to her for a while now, she picked up her book from the bedside table but decided to help herself relax with a hot chocolate, if she could find any.

Peeping out of the door, she looked along the landing. No lights were to be seen and unnervingly, the house had resumed its spookiness in the dark, aided and abetted by the howling. As quietly as she could, so as not to wake Elspeth, she crept down the stairs with only the light from her mobile phone to show her the way. Reaching the bottom, she heard a creak and swung the phone round to shine down the passage.

Tess stopped breathing. In the passage and gliding slowly towards her now was the most awful apparition. It was wearing a long white gown and carrying a candle in one hand. Its hair was flowing wraith-like and its face was as white and waxy as death.

She screamed, long and loud – but was unable to move. The spectre had halted its advance on her but now came nearer and, this was a strange thing, gave Tess 'The Look'. The one that only Elspeth was capable of giving. The night-gowned figure passed her and, turning to give another 'Look' which still managed to permeate through the layer of cold cream she had on her face. Then she tucked her book under her arm, blew out the candle, switched on the hall light and made her way up the stairs.

Tess shook her head to dispel the vision she had just seen. Elspeth would never let her live it down and no wonder. She had screamed like a banshee, for heaven's sake and her aunt hadn't even flinched. Entering the kitchen, she put the light on and searched the cupboards for a bottle of spirits. The alcoholic kind. Her nerves were in shreds and the hot chocolate was now forgotten. As she took her tot of whisky back up to her bedroom, she reflected that she would rather encounter a dozen howling wolves on the moors than another chance midnight meeting with her aunt

Chapter 4

Over the breakfast table the next morning, Tess was pleasantly surprised and relieved that Elspeth didn't mention last night's incident, apart from to ask if she'd been woken up by the howling, which Tess confirmed. After another few minutes' silence, Elspeth spoke again.

'Where are the flowers you brought?'

'In my sitting room' shot back Tess, still aggrieved at her aunt's dismissal of them. She had been so sniffy about the blooms that Tess had taken them where they could be enjoyed. She waited for a Look or a tongue-lashing but remarkably there was only a slight lifting of the corners of her mouth. It could hardly be called a smile but it was the nearest she had come to it. Her aunt went on.

'Well Theresa, as you seem to have been foisted on me by your father, no doubt to the satisfaction of neither of us, we will have to make the best of it. To this end, we have been invited to my friend Gwen's house for morning coffee. I've accepted for both of us.' and with this, she turned the empty shell of her boiled egg upside down, bashed it viciously with her spoon so it caved in and stalked off towards her library.

The most astonishing thing about this pronouncement wasn't the bossiness of it – that was only to be expected – but the fact that Elspeth actually had a friend. Tess had imagined her to be a sour-faced recluse like Hugo had been and the revelation that she had even just the one friend was a bit of a shock.

'Yes, great aunt' she called out at Elspeth's disappearing back. She appeared at the doorway again.

'And don't call me great aunt, even if I am. It makes me feel even more ancient. I suppose you'll have to call me Elspeth.'

'If you call me Tess instead of Theresa - it's a deal.'

A pained look came over her aunt's face.

'If I have to' she said, disappearing once again.

'Same.' Tess shouted after her.

Walking into the hallway when she was sure Elspeth was enthroned in her lair, she saw that a newspaper had been shoved through the letterbox. Not wanting to disturb her aunt and feeling fairly sure she would have seen it as she went to her room, so didn't want it, Tess eased it out quietly and crept to the conservatory with it.

It was light and sunny in there, despite having plants on every available surface. Some vines were climbing up in two of the corners and Mother-in-law's Tongue, Spider plants and Umbrella plants were taking over the tall jardinieres. It was a very pleasant place to take breakfast and she would try it tomorrow. Her aunt would probably be glad to be without her company.

The kitchen was lovely too, in a different way. It was quite dark and the ceiling lights had been on, even on an early June morning. Yet the aga and settle at right angles to each other made it seem cosy as did the long, scratched wood table which was accompanied by various un-matching wooden chairs, no doubt gathered or passed down over the years. The room had a nice, old-fashioned feel to it, it enveloped you in a warmth that the streamlined, modern units back at her gutted and remodelled vicarage home didn't bring.

She read the paper, a local one and then contentedly stared out of the window at the fluffy cloud shadows chasing each other across the moors in the breeze and watched the branches of the apple tree outside the window, sway gently. A man came walking purposefully from the side of the house. He looked to be around her aunt's age and wore old twill trousers, a flat tweed cap and a grey shirt with the sleeves rolled up to reveal brown, weather-beaten arms. He carried a spade and on reaching the central flower bed, proceeded to dig out the flowers that were past their best. Curiosity got the better of her so she went out of the door to have a word.

'Hi, I'm Tess' she said, holding out her hand. The man wiped his hand on his trouser leg before shaking hers.

'Hello Miss, I'm George. I would have known who you were anyway because you've got the Wykeham eyes.'

This was a new one on Tess.

'Do you mean the d'Evreux eyes?' she offered

'No Miss, it's the other side, Miss Wykeham d'Evreux's mother's side of the family. The Wykehams are famous round here and all the females have used the Wykeham in their name. That's where the eyes come from. Very unusual, not seen the likes before, 'cept for you today and your grandmother.'

'Well, this is turning out to be a surprising trip,' she laughed 'and do call me Tess.'

'If you're sure Miss, erm Tess? Miss Wykeham d'Evreux always likes to be addressed formally although I've known her for nigh on fifty years.'

'Yes, she would I expect. It's a wonder you don't have to tip your cap to her and call her Your Ladyship.'

George chuckled but replied,

'She's not as bad as all that, you know. A bit eccentric but her heart's in the right place. Her bark is worse than her bite.'

'Her bark's bad enough for me' said Tess 'but seriously, do you think she's doing alright after her brother's death?'

'Hugo? Oh, I doubt that's put her off her stride. Why do you ask?'

'Because - Oh, what time is it?' she looked at her watch in a panicked manner reminiscent of Alice's White Rabbit and hurried off with apologies and a 'Nice to meet you.' She only had a few minutes to present herself in front of Her Ladyship. She ran up the stairs and changed into a decent flowery blouse and white cotton trousers, ran the brush through her hair, added a touch of lipstick and ran down again. No sign of Elspeth and it was eleven forty-eight.

Suddenly remembering the newspaper, she dashed into the conservatory, picked up the paper and ran back as quietly as she could. She lifted the flap of the letterbox and put the newspaper back in place. Then she stood against the bottom of the staircase. She decided against whistling nonchalantly.

Dead on time, the library door opened, Elspeth reached for a cream cardigan hanging from the coat stand and went to open the front door, removing the newspaper and popping it onto the hall table as she did so. Tess breathed a sigh of relief. As they went out of the door, Elspeth said,

'Did you enjoy the newspaper?'

Tess nodded. Damn the woman, she thought.

Chapter 5

Gwen's house was at the other end of the village, past the green then past some more modern houses set back from the road. They went on down a hill where a small, disused railway station nestled and then up again towards some post-war semis with pebble-dashed facades and neat front gardens. Just before those were two large red brick houses, seemingly out of place in a village built almost entirely out of the local stone.

The one Elspeth stopped outside was half disguised with ivy and there was pink and cream honeysuckle growing round a solidly built wooden porch. There was stained glass in all the top window panels and above the door, which was now being opened by a small woman with her short hair sticking out in tiny spikes. Tess was just trying to decide if this was deliberate or if her hair had a life of its own when the small figure enveloped her in a surprisingly strong bear hug.

'So lovely to see you, my dear! I've always wanted to meet you.'

'Lovely to meet you too, Gwen' said Tess, meaning it as it was a warm welcome furlongs away from the 'welcome' she had received from Elspeth.

They were ushered into a bright sunny living room. There was a coffee table with a large vase filled with fresh flowers placed on it. Aunt and niece exchanged brief, meaningful glances. There were two large settees and a large wing-backed armchair currently occupied by a man, lounging back and weighing her up.

His white shirt covered a muscled chest and his blond hair fell across one side of his brow. His eyes were narrowed, the ice blue showing through thick black lashes. Tess found her eyes wandering down to his legs and thought how tall he would be if he deigned to stand up and unfurl them.

'Dark?' came her aunt's voice from behind her, 'what are you doing here?'

'And how nice to see you too, Batty' he replied with one eyebrow raised.

Tess gasped in horror and cringed as he looked on with amusement. Amazingly, Elspeth didn't turn him into a frog.

'My niece, Theresa' Elspeth could feel the eyes burning into the side of her head, 'or Tess as she prefers to be known for some reason. This is Gwen's grandson.'

Elspeth went to relieve Gwen of the heavy tray containing cups, milk, sugar and a pot of freshly ground coffee by the smell of it, while Gwen scuttled off again, returning with what looked like a home-made cake, drizzled with icing and filled with cream and jam.

Tess sat down on the settee with her generous mouth now set in a tight line. She may have misgivings about her aunt's character but she could never be so rude to her face – even if she dare. If anyone was allowed to be rude to her, it was family, not some condescending, sarcastic man who couldn't even be bothered to get up and greet them or help his grandmother with the coffee tray. Anyway, she thought grumpily, what sort of a stupid, Mills and Boon name was Dark?

'You're still off work then?' Elspeth asked and was rewarded with a slight nod, 'How did you manage to drive here?'

'I've hired an automatic so I don't have to use my left foot' he replied equably.

Puzzled, Tess looked down and noticed the foot was poking from his jeans and encased in plaster. She mentally apologised for her mistake but she still didn't like the man.

Elspeth took the place next to Gwen and leaned across to him, her brows knitted together.

'I don't suppose you have any information? Too trifling a matter for the police, I expect.'

He sighed patronisingly.

'Don't you think we have better things to do with our time, like chasing real criminals. And murderers.'

'No murders round here recently. Have you got many in Whitby, Sherlock?'

He ignored her. Honestly, thought Tess, they're as bad as each other.

'Or that other thing I asked you to find?' Elspeth went on, 'So very recognisable. I suppose that's gone forever too. What good are you?'

'I thought you'd be able to see where it was with your crystal ball, you old witch.'

Tess gasped again and was just about to stand up and tell him what she thought of him when she caught a smile on her aunt's face. It was so unexpected that it almost unnerved her. What's more, Dark's lips twitched and his eyes crinkled with humour. What on earth was going on?

The rest of the time passed in pleasant chit-chat with Tess trying to avoid Dark's gaze although she could feel his eyes on her. The two old friends had a good catch-up even though they apparently saw each other once or twice a week. Gwen paused every five minutes to explain to Tess who the people in question were or where the building being described was and who it belonged to. Her grandson joined in a couple of times but generally just listened, leaning back nonchalantly in his chair. The most embarrassing part was when Gwen said how beautiful she thought Tess was and although Tess didn't expect Dark to agree, she was still affronted when he said nothing at all. Her elfin face and rosebud mouth had been remarked on before- and her long lustrous dark hair before she decided to change it so as not to be like her aunt - but it really boiled down to those 'different' blue eyes, which had ended up being almost as embarrassing as her name.

As her aunt stood up to go, Tess felt nothing but relief. She felt like, to paraphrase Count Adhemar in A Knight's Tale, she had been 'weighed, measured and found wanting' by Gwen's grandson. Gwen was lovely if a little scatty but her grandson was so rude.

Nevertheless, she wouldn't follow his example and would say goodbye politely.

'Goodbye Dark, nice to meet you' Although it really, really wasn't.

'Oh god, not you too' was all the answer she got. Still rude, even after her effort – and what did he mean?

As they took their leave, he threw an envelope on the table and met Elspeth's eyes. She nodded in return and picked it up, putting it into her pocket.

*

As they made their way back to Wykeham Grange, Tess heard a little gurgling noise coming from her aunt's throat and in a panic, tried to bring to mind her first aid course. She soon realised it wasn't needed as the noise had been a laugh of sorts.

'What's funny?' she asked.

'Dark' and the gurgling chuckle escaped again.

'I don't find him funny in the slightest' said Tess with as much hubris as she could muster.

'No, he doesn't give a good first impression, I have to admit – but you called him Dark.' She turned and smiled at a puzzled Tess.

'Well, that's his stupid name, isn't it? That's what you called him?'

'No, his name is Luke.'

Tess stopped walking.

'Then why…?'

'Gwen's surname is Mills as was her son Alun's and her grandson's. Luke is in the police force in Whitby when he's not convalescing, where he is a Detective Sergeant. D.S.Mills. So I call him Dark Satanic Mills. Dark for short. It's just a joke.'

And she'd called him Dark too, she felt such an idiot. No wonder he reacted as he did. Elspeth was still talking.

'Luke is Lukas actually as his mother is Scandinavian. You can probably tell from his Norse colouring – he dressed up as a Viking in our last Folk Festival. She and Luke's father split up and she lives back in Oslo. His father, Gwen's son, died not long after. Gwen continued to bring Lukas up here in the village.'

Tess was still trying to come to terms with Luke demeaning himself enough to dress in costume in public. Although the thought of him dressed as Thor was doing strange things to her. She stopped the train of thought immediately. Another thought popped up.

'But why did he call you Batty? That really was so rude.' she complained.

'Luke and his family lived in the village before the marriage break-up. He was brought up here and went to the local school. I used to invite all the children, every Halloween, to the Folklore Museum and tell them spooky stories.' She illustrated the word 'spooky' by wiggling her fingers in front of Tess. 'I wore a witch's costume with a pointed hat, which had spiders and bats dangling from it. He's called me Batty since he was five years old. Fondly, I hope, although you never know.'

Tess was still trying to process all this.

'Hang on. Folklore Museum? Your Folklore Museum? My dad didn't mention that.'

'We *do* have a lot of catching up to do don't we?'

As they reached the Grange, Tess had an inkling this may be a little more fun than she originally thought.

Chapter 6

To Tess's surprise, Elspeth was seated opposite her at the other side of a white wicker table in the conservatory, just finishing off a breakfast of toast and thick homemade orange marmalade.

When she had suggested breakfast in the conservatory, she hoped her aunt would refuse so she could just enjoy the peace. Her aunt had replied that they could talk in there as well as anywhere else, she supposed, and marched through with the breakfast tray. She had just asked her if she'd slept well and Tess had replied, yes, after the howls had subsided. Elspeth looked up at her but nothing else was said. The sound still sent shivers through Tess but it was probably just an antisocial dog with antisocial owners.

As Elspeth poured another cup of tea for them, Tess studied her. With her fine bone structure, unusual eyes and her silver hair pulled back in an elegant chignon, she was quite a striking-looking woman – as well as being six feet tall, three inches taller than she was herself. Tess couldn't work out why she had found her so frightening on her previous visit until she realised it was the personality, not the looks, that were the cause. She ventured a sentence to break the silence which had now descended.

'What was it you wanted to talk to me about Elspeth?'

'What?' her aunt looked distracted for a moment. 'Ah yes, the Folklore Museum. It was something I started many years ago. You can't live around these parts and ignore the folklore of the area; it is steeped in the rich tales passed down over hundreds of years. I ran it from the large barn in the field next to Hugo's house, actually his field. The old stone building, set back from the road?'

'I'm sorry, I haven't noticed it. I'll have a walk past…'

'I'll give you the key then you can go in and have a look around. Learn about the local myths and legends. Wade the Giant. The Weaver's Tale. The Gytrash of Godesmere.' Here her aunt looked up as though she should know about this.

'What's a Gy -whatever it was?'

'The Gytrash is the local version of the Black Dog stories. You'll find the story in the museum.

You know the Gytrash is there because it howls at night.'

She looked into her niece's eyes, unnervingly identical to her own, to judge her reaction. Those eyes widened.

'You think it's the Gytrash? Couldn't it just be another dog nearby?'

'The howling started the night after Hugo died and has been heard every night since.' Elspeth said meaningfully, although the meaning escaped Tess. She was beginning to think she was back in the Addam Family mansion. She turned the subject around.

'Do you miss him a lot then?' she asked sympathetically. Catching her aunt's puzzled look, she carried on, 'Hugo? Dad said you were really missing him?'

'Hugo?' she said in the manner of Dame Edith Evan's 'A Handbag?', 'I don't miss him at all, miserable old devil. Hardly saw him when he was alive. He didn't like me, even when we were children and the feeling was mutual. We only nodded, briefly, when we passed on one of his rare appearances in the village. The last time we had a pleasant conversation was nearly forty years ago. And that ended in an argument over something or nothing' she added as an afterthought.

'Did Dad get it wrong? Who is it you miss then?

'Barney. Barney the Bichon Frise. Hugo's dog, although it spent as much time with me as it did in that hell hole. It was warmer here and I made a fuss of him, so he used to trot over here every day for a doggie treat and a cuddle. Hugo did like dogs, well, tolerated them but he actively disliked people. He apparently got Barney for a knockdown price as the little zig-zag black mark on his snout prevented him fetching the normal high price these dogs reach.

His nephew stole the dog as well as the ring. Or kicked him out of the house when he took possession, so he ran away. Either way, he's gone. I know he's stolen him though as he's still worth a lot of money and he's under two years old. Not microchipped, of course, my brother didn't believe in all that.

I saw a large house, brick, not stone, on the edge of a village. It had two pointed gables with a smaller, straight bit joining them. It had a large garden. A young girl. A river or stream running nearby, perhaps under a bridge? A hissing noise came to me – and the word 'Green'. Or perhaps the paintwork was green?'. Her aunt's voice trailed off; her eyes unfocused

There were many surprising things about this stream-of-consciousness speech that struck Tess. Not least the fact that her unemotional aunt could go gooey over a little ball of fluff called Barney. Then, accusing the nephew of dog theft – as well as ring theft, whatever this ring was. Then there was the trance-like vision of the house and its location. Was this what Dark/Luke meant when he mentioned a crystal ball? Was she a witch after all?

She shook her head to dispel these silly ideas but felt she needed more information. What was this ring, for example?

'When you say ring…'

'The Balefire ring. It was the reason why Hugo's life was a miserable one because it wasn't his to keep. No time for chit-chat now. Get ready. We're off to Hawkshurst village. It will only take us two hours if we take the moorland road over the top.'

Her aunt bustled off to get ready, leaving Tess open-mouthed. Well, that's my morning planned then, she thought as she went upstairs to fetch a thin jacket and put a smear of lipstick on.

*

Tess collected her car keys from the hall table and went outside to make sure the passenger seat was clear for Elspeth. She noticed a man entering the driveway. He was on the small side with a shock of brown curly hair and big, wide eyes, which all had the unfortunate effect of making him look like Shirley Temple. He held his hand out as he came closer and gave her his best smile.

'Hi, I thought I'd come and introduce myself. I'm your cousin Curwen – and you must be…'

'Tess' and she stepped forward to shake his hand, pulling back as though she'd been shot when she heard an autocratic voice behind her.

'You're not her cousin.'

He looked unabashed as though he was used to the derogatory treatment, while Tess would have sunk willingly into the ground to escape.

'Good morning aunt' he said with a smile. Nevertheless, his top lip was quivering. He didn't fool anyone, thought Tess, he was terrified of Elspeth too.

'I'm not your aunt either. Kindly remove yourself from my driveway.'

Tess looked on in silent horror as Curwen lifted his eyebrows as nonchalantly as he could manage and pretended to saunter off when his whole body language betrayed the fact that he wanted to exit the driveway at a brisk trot.

Tess turned to fix Elspeth with a stare that conveyed the horror and sheer embarrassment she felt. However, her aunt was already on the way to the separate stone building to the side of the house.

'You won't need your car,' she shot back over her shoulder, 'I'm driving us.'

Tess closed her eyes amidst visions of a little old, black Ford Popular, covered in cobwebs, being backed out of the garage. She wasn't at all sure she fancied being driven along narrow moorland roads and steep and winding valleys at 10 miles per hour by a maiden aunt who probably only drove on Sundays. And then only in the summer months.

The sigh that seemed to come up from the soles of her feet was interrupted by a loud revving from the garage. Tess imagined the revving intensifying on the journey as Elspeth tried to change from first gear to second, failing miserably. Well, if all else failed, they could probably get out and walk, it would probably be quicker.

This train of thought was interrupted by the sight of a sleek red sports car backing out towards her. She just managed to catch the name, Porsche Boxster, as it shot past her in a cloud of dust.

As she was debating with what little of her mind remained whether an old vintage car or a racy sports car was safer, her aunt's voice interrupted.

'Well, get in then!'

*

The door handle was being held in a grip of iron, as was the edge of the bucket seat at the other side. Tess's feet were both permanently jammed against imaginary brakes and her back was pushed right into the seat.

She closed her eyes as her aunt hurtled along narrow country roads and up and down steep inclines because, if she opened them, she got the impression of one of those old silent movies where everything is speeded up to an impossible rate, four times as fast as it should be. She vaguely wondered if there were any sick bags in the glove compartment for any unsuspecting and unwilling passengers.

Just as she thought it was safe to open her eyes as it felt to be a straight road, her aunt swerved to avoid a giant pothole, smoothly taking all four wheels on the grass verge and off again without once losing speed. Tess thought it might take two full days to unclench her hands – and her teeth.

Ahead of them now was a large lorry, a petrol tanker. The road was straight but still narrow and her aunt didn't appear to be slowing down. An involuntary whimper escaped from Tess's lips as the car pulled out to overtake. The lorry driver looked on in astonishment at the old lady overtaking him and at the girl, pressed against the passenger window who seemed to be mouthing 'Help' – her eyes as big as his son's frisbees.

All this time, Elspeth had been carrying on a sporadic, one-sided conversation of which Tess hadn't heard a word. Tess knew it wasn't the wind noise from the open roof that was to blame for her temporary deafness, it was sheer, raw terror.

Elspeth was saying something to her now and with a mounting horror, Tess realised she was rummaging in her pocket, from which she produced an envelope, handing it across. Tess snatched it, desperate for her aunt to return her other hand to the steering wheel but she didn't even attempt to read it. She could feel 'The Look' boring into her skull but Tess kept her eyes on the road, reasoning that at least one of them ought to.

Very soon, they reached the outskirts of a large village and Elspeth began to slow down. As Tess was trying to work out why a journey that took half as long as it should have done actually felt like it had taken five times as long as it did…the car pulled into a small car park next to a café.

'Tea?' asked Elspeth brightly.

'Whisky. Double.' croaked Tess.

'What is *wrong* with you girl?' her aunt said, marching ahead into the café.

*

'The colour's returning to your cheeks, you were as pale as a ghost' said Elspeth with obvious glee.

'To be fair,' Tess felt the need to justify herself, 'I have never been driven on country roads in an adapted spaceship at the speed of light by a geriatric Flash Gordon before.'

'Nonsense – I never once went over the speed limit. It just felt fast because you were lower to the ground and because of the type of roads they were but I know these roads, remember, and I don't take risks, only calculated manoeuvres. I have also taken two advanced driving courses, the last only two years ago. I just wanted to make sure my skills hadn't abandoned me at my 'geriatric' age but I actually came top out of the lot of them, everyone being much younger than me. I have the certificate to prove it. Have you always been a scaredy-cat?'

'No!' Tess was stung, although she knew she wasn't a very brave person both physically and in life's decisions. She wouldn't admit it though. 'It just wasn't what I expected, that's all.'

Suddenly remembering, she brought out a tightly squashed envelope from her pocket.

'Did you want me to read this?' she asked and as there was no answer, she did so.

There were two pieces of paper inside, the larger one on white notepaper said 'All I could manage I'm afraid Batty. One of the constables whom I'd asked to keep his ear to the ground said that he'd been talking in the pub to someone. It might help and I'm sure you'll use your 'witchy powers' to find Barney. Good luck. L.'

Tess looked up.

'Quite rude again. 'Witchy powers?''

Elspeth dismissed it and urged her to carry on.

Tess picked up the second paper which had fallen from the first. It was on lined notebook paper, the writing in a different hand, not as neat as the first. 'Heard down the Malt Shovel last night of a little dog that had just appeared. It apparently looks like a cuddly toy on a lead and is being walked in the streets of Hawkshurst village. No names or address but could be your man. Or dog!'

'So here we are' said Elspeth. 'Drink up – we're going to get Barney back.'

Questions came to mind but Tess's system wasn't yet capable of forming them into coherent sentences, so she just drank up and followed her aunt outside.

Chapter 7

Elspeth looked around her, closed her eyes slowly, then snapped them open and made her way down a hill towards the edge of the village.

'Do you know where you're going?' asked Tess.

'Yes' came the reply and Tess suddenly remembered her aunt's description she had given this morning over breakfast. Where she thought she would find Barney. That must have been some sort of a dream though, surely? She could have been remembering a place she had seen before.

'Have you been to this village before ?' she asked.

'I have passed by it on the top road many times and Gwen and I have called at the Tea Rooms a few times. But never down this end of the village,' she added, possibly realising why Tess had asked.

'You must have known there was a river though?'

'I was aware there was a river flowing through at least two or three of the villages but have never actually seen it. This part isn't visible from the Tea Rooms.' Elspeth was looking disgruntled at being tested on her 'vision'.

After a few more minutes, during which Tess had wisely kept silent, they reached a triangle of grass at the bottom of the hill. There were four large houses set round it and to their left was an old stone bridge, an ancient packhorse bridge. Tess left Elspeth for a moment and walked up to it. Underneath ran a fast-flowing stream, which was probably a tributary to the main river.

At the other side of the bridge was an old Station house belonging to a single-track railway line, running parallel with the stream. It looked disused but according to the information board, this was 'Hawkshurst Station. Steam Train running twice a day from April to October.' Turning back, she noticed a pull-in for about four or five cars at the other side of the river and looking beyond it, she saw Elspeth.

She was staring up at the largest of the houses, set further back from the road than the others. It had two gable ends, joined by a lower part with a pantile roof, an old dormer window poking from it. As she followed her aunt through the low wooden gate and up the garden path, Tess saw the name 'Low Green Lodge' written on a slate plaque next to the solid front door. Green? This has to be a coincidence, she thought. Tess was firmly in the 'won't believe until proved' camp which was how she usually dealt with any New Age nonsense.

'What on earth are you going to say to them?' she whispered.

'Trust me, keep quiet and try to look intelligent' replied Elspeth, rattling the door knocker.

There was no answer and Tess was all for creeping away but her aunt rapped again as loud as she could. This time, although the door remained closed, a pleasant-looking lady with wavy brown hair appeared from round the side of the house to their left.

'Sorry,' she smiled 'have you been knocking long? We were in the garden.'

'Do forgive us calling on you unexpectedly.' Elspeth was putting her best cut-glass accent on. 'We were in the Tea Rooms and someone mentioned you had just bought a Bichon Frise? As I myself am thinking of getting one as a companion when my niece isn't here, I thought I would be incredibly cheeky and ask how you find them, behaviour-wise? I would prefer a breed with a gentle temperament.'

'Oh, that will have been Ethel – or her daughter Jayne perhaps? They absolutely adore Pip.'

Pip? New name or wrong dog? Contrasting with Elspeth's supreme confidence, Tess felt like crawling for shelter and staying there till it was all over.

'So, I *have* come to the right house?'

'Yes, you have. Please do follow me. Pip is with my daughter. They bonded as soon as we bought him and he won't leave her side. He protects her, we like to think.'

As they reached the back of the house, a long, wide garden stretched before them. A summerhouse was just in sight at the bottom end, with ornamental trees set around it.

The woman indicated a patio behind the house and in front of a long, open bi-fold door was a young girl in a wheelchair. She would be about twelve years old and there, sitting bolt upright on her lap, was a small white dog. Her mother explained to her about Elspeth's errand and the girl smiled – a genuine smile like her mother's – and said,

'We can recommend them, can't we Mum? Pip is such a good little dog. He's so happy, he makes me feel happy too. He looks after me!' and mother and daughter exchanged looks which said they both absolutely believed this to be true.

Suddenly, Pip jumped down from the girl's lap and trotted over to Elspeth who crouched down to meet him.

'Hello, little fellow' she crooned in a most un-Elspeth – like voice.

The dog put its front paws on her knees and both dog and woman looked at each other silently for a long time, when nobody seemed to breathe in case they broke the communion. Then Elspeth gave the barest nod and Pip leant forward to lick her nose before trotting back to his place on the girl's knee, jumping up lightly and effortlessly.

'Well!' said the woman in amazement.

'You're very honoured' laughed the girl by way of explanation, 'he normally ignores strangers.'

'He sticks his nose in the air and refuses to leave Naomi for anyone' her mother added, laughing now.

Elspeth got up slowly, her eyes still on Pip. She walked slowly over to the girl; her features arranged in a serious expression.

Oh no, thought Tess. She couldn't bear to witness the next scene. Her aunt stroked the dog's head again and then addressed the girl, Naomi.

'I have to say this…' she began and Tess started to turn away. She didn't want to be part of it. Her aunt continued,

'…that after seeing what a good and clever little dog Pip is, and how much he loves you; I am definitely going to buy one.'

'You won't regret it' said the woman as her daughter buried her face in Pip's fur, telling him he was the best dog ever.

'Have you got the name of the breeder? I'd quite like one from the same pedigree.' Her aunt had come over all business-like after casting a glance at her grand-niece who had turned to jelly and was gulping and biting down on her lip hard.

'Ah well, I'm afraid that my husband met him in the pub. He was on his way back from the house where he'd originally sold Pip, somewhere near Durham. The owner had died and her family couldn't take him, so we just found him at the right time. We've always said it was fate that brought him to us' she smiled, looking across at Pip.

'I'm sure you're right' agreed Elspeth 'Did you get his…?'

'Oh sorry, no. I'm afraid not. With him travelling back with Pip, he hadn't brought any official papers with him. We gave him our address and he said he'd send details on but we haven't heard from him. Perhaps he lost the address but we don't need proof of pedigree, just Pip. We do have proof of purchase though as he was rather an expensive little dog and he signed it Hugo Bellweather. Perhaps you could make enquiries?'

Elspeth was frowning, as was Tess. Hugo? If this was a coincidence, it was a strange one. Perhaps Pip wasn't Barney after all, thought Tess but just then, as if he could read her thoughts, he turned to look at her and she saw the zig-zag black mark on his snout.

'I wonder if it's the same breeder I was talking to a few weeks ago. Thick-set, big ox of a man, black greased back hair?'

'Oh no, the exact opposite I'm afraid! This one was small, young, curly brown hair and with an angelic-looking face,' she laughed apologetically.

'Not at all' said Elspeth, 'it's obviously not the right man'

As they waved and shouted their sincere thanks, Tess chanced a look at her aunt on the walk back to the car. Elspeth's eyes were narrowed to slits, her mouth was set and her jaw twitched. They both knew it was *exactly* the right man. Tess would not want to be in Curwen's shoes now for all the tea in China.

Chapter 8

Breakfast the next morning with her aunt, was a silent affair. Elspeth had withdrawn into her own sacred sitting room the previous evening and hadn't been seen again until just now.

Tess hadn't woken up during the night so she wondered aloud if the howling had stopped.

'No' answered Elspeth in a distracted way, frown lines appearing above the arched brows ' it was there but not as loud. Weaker.'

Elspeth seemed lost in her own world and as Tess didn't fancy being embroiled in a Curwen/Elspeth duel to the death, she got up from the table, collecting the tray.

'Would it be alright if I had a look at the museum this morning?'

'What? Yes, of course. Keys are in the hall stand drawer. Marked 'Barn'.' Elspeth went back to her thoughts.

As Tess stepped out onto the road, she looked over to the Green and saw the small figures of two donkeys over the far side near Berry's cottage, nibbling the grass already well-cropped by the wandering sheep.

She turned to her right on the road out of the village. A hundred yards away, she saw the barn standing well back from the road on the left. An iron rod stuck out, bearing an empty chain at either end, which swung unhappily from above the black-painted double doors at the front. There was no sign attached so she supposed her aunt didn't want to invite questions about it and if it would be opening at all? A sign in the window, half-covered in ivy said 'Closed'. It all had a sad, neglected air about it.

Tess went up a dirt track by the side of the barn, grass growing high in the middle of it. The old stone building went quite a way back and she could see some dusty windows high up on the wall. Behind it was a small courtyard and some hard standing which could have been a rough and ready small car park for the museum. This was fenced in with woven fencing and behind that was a long field of grass, stretching right up to the treeline which was effectively a small linear wood of hardy beech, hornbeam and hawthorn, providing a barrier against the prevailing winds from the moors. Through the trees could just be seen a vast expanse of moorland, rising upwards in a gradual incline. All this land belonged to Hugo d'Evreux and now to Curwen. She could see the black chimneys of Rook Hall rising above another line of trees to her right, which followed the field's perimeter.

Returning to the barn doors, she unlocked one, which made a cringe-inducing scraping noise as she pulled it back over stones and lumpy ground. It was dark inside but the switch on the nearest wall didn't want to work. Not wanting to fry herself with dodgy old electrics, she just propped the door open for more light and entered.

With her phone's torch, she could see a line of glass cases along each side, all with artefacts in them. As her eyes got used to the inside, the light from the high, almost opaque windows began to filter through and she could see more clearly.

Part of an old dismantled beam was in a tall glass case. The label said it had been taken from the now-demolished Critty Cottage in the village. It showed a sepia print of a low, whitewashed cottage with a shaggy thatched roof. The beam had witch's marks on it, to turn away evil and protect the house. There was also a list of named witches in the area who had been taken for 'trial'.

Further along was a print of a giant hurling a boulder as big as he was, at another giant. There was also a terrifyingly graphic print of The

Nightmare Horse of Newby, complete with wild, red eyes and flying black mane and tail. She peered to read the description. It was no good, she would have to come back here again when she discovered how to turn the lights on.

Meanwhile, on the counter at the front, she had passed a pile of books in a small wood and glass box on the counter. Going back to have a look, she found the small key on her set of keys fitted neatly into the box and she pulled out 'Folklore, Myths and Legends of the North Yorkshire Moors' by Elspeth Wykeham   d'Evreux.' An author, no less. She put the copy in her bag to read at home.

After a struggle, she managed to close the door and lock up. Curiosity got the better of her and she went a little further across the road until she reached Rook Hall. It was hidden from the road by a large collection of shrubs which had been allowed to grow wild and were all small tree size now. She entered the driveway stealthily, hiding herself behind a tree. The hall was built in a dark grey stone, unlike the lovely mellow stone of most of the village houses. There was a central section with a square gabled tower then longer wings on either side each with large chimneys at either end. The unshuttered windows presenting a stark, black face towards the front. She half expected to see a pale, ghostly face peering through one of the uppermost windows and kept her gaze firmly on the ground floor. She had thought her aunt's house was going to be a forbidding, haunted house when in reality, it was here in front of her.

She shuddered, rubbing her arms although it was a warm day and with one last look, turned her back on the building. How could Curwen live there by himself? She knew she was given to flights of fancy but it was not a happy house.

As she tried to shake off the gloom that had enveloped her, she saw that the donkeys had now been joined by Berry and thankfully made her way over to the Green for a bit of normality and sunshine. A few sheep nibbled the grass near Clover and Daisy, all at ease in each other's company. Berry was lifting up one of the donkey's hooves, using a hoof pick to prise stones and packed mud out of it. She looked up and smiled.

'Come to help?'

'Er – no,' Tess looked alarmed, 'just came to see you.'

'I'll be five minutes then we'll go in and have a cuppa. How is it living with the Dra...Miss Wykeham d'Evreux?' Berry grinned.

'Surprisingly, it's better than I imagined but if she ever offers to drive you anywhere, please don't take her up on it.'

Berry laughed and gave her a running commentary on examples of Elspeth's driving, which were legendary in the village.

'By the way' began Tess as a thought struck her, 'the field behind the old folklore museum – the grass is long and green. These two would have a supply of food for a while. Why don't you ask Curwen?'

A black look crossed Berry's face.

'The same thought occurred to me but when I asked your cousin, he said he was looking to sell and didn't want potential purchasers treading in donkey-doos.' She raised her eyes heavenwards and Tess frowned.

'He's not my cousin' and realised she was echoing Elspeth's words. 'I don't suppose Hugo ever let you…?'

'You're joking aren't you?' Her pretty, rosy cheeks spread out in a grin. 'Your aunt tried to get him to see sense as it would help to keep the grass down. Hugo said he would rather pay George -a pittance- once a month to keep the grass reasonable than be seen doing what amounted to a good deed,'

'He sounds delightful. My aunt asked?' she frowned again at the disparity between the dragon aunt of earlier recollections and the one here and now. Although, thinking of her attachment to Barney, maybe it shouldn't be a surprise.

'Yes, she was great actually, even if I am scared to death of her. Now – that cuppa. Or …how do you fancy sampling the delights of our local pub? Des, the landlord has a bit of land at the back. I'm working on him, you never know.'

'Sounds good to me. I haven't been inside yet.'

They ambled across the Green towards the ancient-looking Wykeham Arms and just before they reached the low wooden door with an old ring-handled latch on it, Tess paused.

'This isn't the type of village pub where you go in and all the locals turn round and stare at you, is it? Like you've personally brought the Black Death to their hostelry? Then do they stay quiet the rest of the time, like they've been talking about you and had to stop when you walked in?

Berry's infectious laugh rang out.

'Don't be daft, you've been watching too many old films' and she pushed Tess in front of her into the bar. All the people on bar stools and at tables turned round to look at her. Conversation seized. Tess squeaked and looked across at Berry who was doubled up.

'Come on, you drama queen, let me introduce you.'

One by one, she went round the early lunchtime customers and they were all lovely and friendly. Everyone is nosy when someone walks into a pub, aren't they? reasoned Tess. She had done the same herself on many occasions.

They had just reached a tall, slim figure with broad shoulders and jeans encasing snake hips. He wore a black V-necked tee shirt showing off his muscular arms and well-toned body. Luke! Tess took an involuntary step backwards while Berry forged ahead.

'Tess, this is…'

'We've met' came his short, sharp reply but the ice-blue eyes were full of amusement, possibly at Tess's reaction. She swallowed and stepped forward.

'Luke' she said pleasantly as she forced a smile. He responded with a genuine smile, showing perfect white teeth.

'Well, as you've managed to get my name right, can I buy you a drink? You too Berry?'

'Thank you, just a lime and soda please' Berry said over her shoulder, noticing the landlord was on his own. 'I just have to see a man about two donkeys.'

'Same for me please' whispered Tess as Luke's lips twitched and he turned, calling the barmaid over, who looked delighted to be summoned.

Chapter 9

Passing Tess's drink over to her, Luke picked his up and indicated the door.

'Shall we sit outside, it's a shame to waste the sun.'

'Had we better wait for Berry?' she asked, suddenly nervous for reasons she didn't want to think about.

He looked over and smiled.

'I think she may be a while yet.'

Indeed, Berry and Des the landlord seemed to be getting on extremely well, leaning in to each other and laughing. Hmm, thought Tess, she might not even notice we've gone. She followed Luke outside, where the sudden glare made her blink. It was very dark inside the pub apart from all the corner lamps throwing a yellow light just below them. It was so old, with beams, inglenooks and small, low windows but she could imagine it would be very cosy and welcoming in

71

winter when the fire was lit. They sat down at a picnic bench overlooking the green.

'How's Batty?'

Tess pursed her lips.

'You don't like me calling her that, do you?'

'I know the story of why you do but it just sounds so disrespectful.'

'Typical vicar's daughter' teased Luke, 'Elspeth doesn't mind me calling her that occasionally and yes, I do usually call her Elspeth. When I called her Batty at my gran's, your expression could have curdled milk so I thought I'd give it another go.'

He was laughing at her. Amusement shone from his eyes as he turned his full attention on her.

'You like winding people up don't you' she said huffily, blushing under his gaze.

'When I'm assured of a satisfying reaction like yours, I certainly do. Shall we start again? My name's Luke and I'm a policeman.' He grinned at her, holding out his hand. She felt his firm grip.

'My name's Tess and I'm – well I'm nothing at the moment' she finished lamely.

'I wouldn't say that' he replied, causing another of Tess's increasingly frequent blushes. 'What *did* you do then?'

'I worked in accountancy' she grimaced, waiting for the inevitable comment of 'how boring'. 'I was made redundant a month ago and haven't found another job yet. To tell you the truth, I don't know what I want to do yet as long as it doesn't involve accountancy. I'm at a crossroads in my life I think but there are no signposts there to indicate the choices.

She took a long drink from her glass and was glad she hadn't ordered something alcoholic or she would be telling him her life story soon and crying into her beer. Luke leaned back to get a better look at her and narrowed his eyes.

'What do you want to do as opposed to what you think you *ought* to do?

'My mind is blank. I have brain fog. I would like it to do something creative which is definitely more my style but as to what…?' she raised her hands in a helpless gesture.

'You're not staying here then?'

'No, just till Elspeth is better. Better from what I don't know because my father, her nephew, thought she was struggling with Hugo's death but apparently she isn't. It was Barney she was missing. Are you living here with your gran?'

'Almost' he laughed. 'She's been looking after me while my leg heals properly and they accept me back on the force. Nothing exciting – broke it

73

in the line of duty through jumping over a wall after a thief. I've watched too many detective programmes. I wouldn't mind staying there though as she spoils me rotten and the thought of going back to a second-storey, impersonal flat doesn't thrill me. Elspeth phoned my gran last night with the whole tale of Barney. She is an old softy occasionally – she just does a great job of disguising it.'

'I'm coming to realise that' she smiled, then stiffened as he leant in towards her.

'Has she mentioned Hugo's death to you?'

'I know he fell down the stairs? No, nothing else. Why?' she asked as she saw him frown.

'She didn't say I was convinced that nephew of hers had murdered him?'

'Oh good god no! You're joking! No of course you're not. I know she doesn't like him but why would you think that? Was there any doubt? I thought it was an accident.'

'That's what an investigation and the coroner said so I have to be ruled by that but there was just something shifty about him. You get a feel for these things after watching so many people lie in my job. I'm sure Curwen Aberford was lying when he said he hadn't been there but it was just a gut feeling. Everything else pointed to it being an accident so I just have to accept it. His girlfriend in Darlington gave him an alibi for that night and it stands up. I just have a feeling that he contributed towards Hugo's death.'

'Contributed? You didn't say murder though?'

'Contributed was actually Elspeth's word. There's nothing I could make stick in a court of law and she made me promise to drop it but I am going to make it so uncomfortable round here for that preening, cocky little …Harpo Marx – that he will be glad to leave.'

'Elspeth's word? You've told her your suspicions?'

'Yes and she dismissed them. She has 'seen' the incident and says Curlylocks only 'contributed' in a non-intentional way to his death. Unfortunately, and keeping this fact from my hardened and practical colleagues, I have to believe her.'

'You do? Why?'

'Because when Elspeth 'sees' an event, you can be fairly sure there's a 99% chance she is right.'

'You can't honestly believe in all that?' laughed Tess incredulously, 'I wouldn't have thought you were the type.'

'When you've known Elspeth all your life then you believe in it. She's told my family and others in the village things that no one else could possibly have known. Things that have proved to be true. Lost things found. Theories proved beyond doubt.

I used to think it was trickery. I thought like you do, that it was a load of old cobblers. Yet time and time again she has proved me wrong. If I don't believe in anything else, I believe in Elspeth. My gran says Elspeth's mother was just the same – and her grandmother too.'

Tess took a minute to digest this. The world had gone mad. The village had just been resurrected in her mind as the 'lighted torches and pitchforks' kind of village that believed in the 'Old Ways' – and the handsome, reliable hero had just been turned into one of the local witch's henchmen. He just didn't seem the sort. Luke studied her expression.

'She was right about the dog wasn't she?' he said and Tess grudgingly agreed in her mind but not out loud, while still holding out for the comfort of coincidence in that matter. There was a silence for a few seconds before Tess said,

'Harpo Marx?'

'Look him up' replied Luke

'I know who he is.' Tess threw back and they both grinned. Still smiling, Luke caught Tess's eye and they stayed still for a moment, Tess hardly daring to breathe.

Just then, the barmaid came over with a plate of sandwiches and a dazzling smile, both exclusively for Luke. Tess felt a hand on her shoulder and turned to see a miserable-looking Berry.

'Have you got time for a cuppa at mine? I can do you a sandwich too?' she said, eyeing the plate in front of Luke. 'Des has turned me down.'

'Bit forward Berry, asking him to marry you.'

'Oh shut up Luke.' Berry shot back good-naturedly and he laughed.

Why can't I be more like that and say what I feel, thought Tess as she followed Berry across the green. It was no good, she thought, looking back at the Norse god that was Luke, lounging back with his eyes screwed up against the sun, she turned to jelly every time he fixed her with his eyes. Why didn't her heart and body do what her mind told them to?

Chapter 10

There was no refusal of marriage for Berry, only a very reluctant refusal of donkey-housing ground at the back of the pub.

Des was very apologetic but said he needed that back patch of grass as a safe area for customers with children and dogs as it is fenced in. Apart from the part where the benches and tables were actually concreted into the ground, the grass area wasn't any bigger than her garden really. Berry didn't blame him at all. She'd have excused him anything judging by her beatific expression when she talked about him.

Tess had retired to bed early. Her aunt was still in an unsociable mood and she realised that leaving her to her thoughts, whatever they may be, was the best thing to do. She now rested against three plumped-up pillows with the rose print duvet covering her knees like a tent, with

Elspeth's 'Folklore, Myths and Legends' book propped up there. She turned to The Gytrash of Godesmere.

*

A few hours later Tess woke up suddenly and sat bolt upright in bed. As soon as her mind adjusted to her surroundings, everything became crystal clear. She knew now. She felt it and she had to do something about it urgently because she knew why the howling had stopped.

A loud crash of thunder shook the house to its foundations and a flash of lightning lit up the bedroom through the curtains. She could hear the rain throwing itself against the window in abandon. Squeezing her eyes tightly to shut all rational thought out, she flung the duvet back, putting on her warmest clothes and the most waterproof coat she had brought. Moving silently along the landing so as not to wake Elspeth, she descended the stairs and grabbed a sausage roll from the kitchen. Then she very quietly opened the front door, locking it safely behind her.

With the key in her pocket, she tried to avoid the gravel which may have alerted her aunt, although the noise of the storm should cover any incidental noises out here. She kept to the sodden grass edges until she reached the road, where she turned right.

She was soaked to the skin in seconds. She ran towards Rook Hall, pulling her hood down over her eyes. She stopped on the way at the barn door but she had been there earlier and knew it was empty. Running on to the Hall, she saw that Curwen's car was there but all the lights were out, making it look even more forbidding. She found her way to the back and risked switching on the torch she had snatched up at the last minute. There was a door at the back that had a rickety porch attached but the outside door of it was locked. She shone the torch at the floor inside but couldn't see any movement.

Conscious that time was of the essence, she ran, slipping and sliding, up to the shed she could see in the distance. After doing a spectacular slide on the muddy grass, she reached the door and rattled it. She realised this wasn't the place she wanted either, it wouldn't be locked.

Reaching the road again, she looked back to her bedroom window, trying to gauge the distance between that and the place she needed to be. She battled her way onto the moor which lay behind Wykeham Grange. It was pitch black but she wouldn't have been able to see anything anyway as the rain was driving at her horizontally. She blinked and tried to wipe the deluge away from her eyes. About half a mile along the road a suffused light, presumably from a hidden moon, appeared and the moorland took on a surreal appearance. The light particles were hanging just above the ground to give a misty appearance, with huge, rolling black clouds climbing up into the sky above it. Occasionally, a flash of lightning made strange alien shapes on the saturated landscape around her.

She lifted her head in despair. Now and then she could make out a grey, still mass against a bluff or an outcrop of rock but the sheep weren't moving from their shelter and didn't respond to her desperate voice. 'Come ON!' she shouted in desperation. It was summer but she was shivering uncontrollably. The sausage roll was disintegrating in her pocket but she brought it out for one last time. It was no good, it was a fool's errand. Very reluctantly she made her way home, thinking guiltily about a warm, dry bed.

She reached the Grange, not caring about the noise on the gravel any more. As she approached the temporary sanctuary of the porch, she let out a cry of alarm and sprang back. There, under the porch was a large figure, all in black, a hood pulled low over its face. It was the early hours of the morning – this couldn't be happening!

Tess stood there, frozen in terror, until the silent figure slowly turned its face towards her.

The features seemed almost recognisable, although obscured with the amount of rain waterfalling from a brimmed hat under the hood. Was it Aunt Elspeth? What in God's name…! It all became much clearer when she was on the receiving end of the Look to end all Looks – obscured by rain or not. Not a word was spoken until Tess stepped up to her.

'What are you doing out here in this weather?' shouted Tess above the hammering of rain on the porch roof. It seemed a reasonable enough question.

'I felt like a shower but forgot the soap.' There was a pause. 'You locked the door'

'But- Yes- But you were inside.'

A deep sigh made itself felt rather than heard and a weary voice said.

'Can we go in?'

This was bizarre but the words made Tess spring into action and, diving in her pocket for the key as the remains of the sausage roll dripped onto the ground, she unlocked the door.

'What's that?' asked her aunt, hesitating at the door.

'It was a sausage roll' came the inadequate reply.

She followed her aunt's rainy trail into the kitchen where there was warmth from the Aga and a chance to dry their clothes.

'I am so sorry' Tess apologised as Elspeth stood with her back to her facing the Aga in an ominous silence. 'I locked the door behind me for safety's sake. I had no idea you would be out in this weather. Why *were* you?'

'Why were *you*?' asked the voice, still facing away from her. How to explain this?

'You probably won't believe this but I woke up suddenly and just knew. I knew beyond any doubt that the howling stopped because it wasn't the Gytrash of Godesmere but a stray dog that had probably been fed by Hugo before he died and now it would be starving. I went to try and find it, saw an old feeding bowl in the porch at the back of the Hall- and knew I was right. The shed was locked so it couldn't have sheltered in there so I went out onto the moors to look, hoping it had found a shelter under the rocks like the sheep do but…'

She tailed off as Elspeth turned round, producing a black, soaking wet bundle from inside her coat. It was a dog, not much bigger than Barney but much thinner and its fur was stuck to its body. It wasn't moving. It wasn't even shivering which worried Tess more than anything.

'Oh no! Is it…?'

'There's a very faint heartbeat. In that cupboard over there you'll find some old travel rugs. Bring them over in front of the Aga.'

Tess ran over, dripping and cold but not caring. She brought them over and put them on the floor in front of the small oven door. Elspeth very carefully dried the dog off as much as she could then lay the inert little body on the bundle of blankets, carefully tucking it in.

'Warm some milk can you?' she asked Tess without taking her eyes off the dog. Tess did so, putting it in a bowl. She reached in the drawer for a teaspoon, holding it up, then getting a nod from Elspeth, brought them over and set them down on the floor.

'Where did you find it?' asked Tess quietly.

In the stand of trees at the back of the museum field. I knew it would afford a little shelter and made for that. I found it in a little hollow where it had probably lain for two days. I was surprised to find a trace of a heartbeat but where there's life, there's hope.' There was a short pause as Elspeth tried to spoon milk into the dog's slack mouth. 'You say you 'felt' it? You knew it was a stray?'

'Yes. Just don't ask me to explain how. How did *you* know?'

'The same' came Elspeth's reply.

Tess was too exhausted to take it all in.

'Get yourself to bed Tess, there's nothing more you can do here.'

'I can stay with it.'

'No, I will be quite comfy in my chair next to the range once I've changed my clothes. Now go on.'

Tess went reluctantly upstairs to have a warm shower and try to sleep. The last thing she saw was Elspeth kneeling next to the little black bundle, talking very gently and trying to coax some milk down its throat.

When the kitchen door had shut, the little dog slowly opened its eyes a fraction. Elspeth saw fear, yet trust as well. More importantly, she saw a glimmer, a tiny spark and as they looked at each other, she knew that everything would be alright.

Chapter 11

When Tess came down to the kitchen the next morning, full of trepidation, she found her aunt asleep on the chair, her arms across the still figure on her knee. Still no movement thought Tess.

She tried to fill the kettle as noiselessly as she could but saw her aunt's head jerk up. Then, miraculously, she saw the dog lift its head up too and when Elspeth bent down, it licked her, very gently on the nose. Great aunt and niece looked at each other with delighted grins on their faces.

'Well that's a good sign of recovery' laughed Tess, thinking how small dogs totally transformed her aunt. It was a shame larger nieces didn't have the same effect.

'She's got a long way to go yet' whispered Elspeth, obviously having ascertained the dog's gender earlier.

Just then came the sound of the front door being opened. Had Tess forgotten to lock it? Did Shep come in today to clean and prepare dinner?

The sound of two male voices nearing the kitchen made Tess look questioningly at her aunt who smiled as the men entered, the younger one still limping slightly.

'Hello Luke, thanks for getting Mr. Grafton for me. Here is your patient sir.' She lifted the dog onto the remaining blanket on the floor, where the patient looked round at everyone then put her head on her paws as though it was too heavy for her neck.

'My niece, Tess – Mr.Grafton, the vet'. Elspeth quickly introduced them and the vet threw her a 'pleased to meet you' before kneeling in front of the dog. Tess was fascinated by the elderly gentleman. His hair and beard were a mixture of dark grey and silver, as was his huge handlebar moustache. It was topped off by a pair of gold-rimmed spectacles perched halfway down his nose. He reminded Tess very much of a short-sighted Miniature Schnauzer.

She smiled to herself, turning back to the kettle and only remembered Luke when she saw him leaning nonchalantly against the dresser, smiling at her with one eyebrow raised. What had he found to amuse him this time, she thought, before she realised she stood before him in a skimpy, pink, low-cut vest and fuchsia-pink pyjama trousers with Little Mermaid prints all over them. Wanting to run straight back upstairs but instead, mustering whatever dignity she had left, she asked,

'Does anyone want a cup of tea?' and walked across to the worktop, arms folded over her chest.

There was a chorus of 'Yes please', with various instructions regarding milk and sugar. Tess handed out the teas, then Luke's mug over to him and got a grin in return. Ignoring it, she asked why he had brought the vet instead of Elspeth just phoning.

'I stayed at my flat in Whitby last night and when your aunt couldn't get a reply early on before the surgery opened, she phoned me and asked me to go round there. Apparently the vet had walked in the back door as I hammered on the front. He'd been tending a sick bull at Bradwin's farm and there was no mobile reception. I know it, it's like a throwback to the forties. They haven't got a tv either. '

She murmured her thanks as he took a sip of the hot tea.

'Has the rain finally stopped?' She had come straight down to the kitchen on waking and had forgotten about the storm in her concern for the abandoned dog.

'It has. It's beautiful out there' he replied, 'the rain has made it a country idyll with wonderfully green grass and leaves – and the surrounding moors are shimmering with the budding of purple heather.'

Tess turned to him in surprise.

'Very poetic' she said.

'I have a poet's heart' he responded with another grin, his right hand in a fist over his chest.

She lifted her eyes to heaven just as Mr. Grafton spoke.

'Hypothermia mostly – made worse by weakness caused by starvation. I imagine she has been feeding on what she can find on the moors and from water in puddles and ditches. She probably kept away from the village which is a shame as someone could have helped her.

I would imagine the only experience of people she has had in the past, is that of being turfed out of a car on the moors and left to fend for herself. She's too weak to be scared at the moment and by the time she has come round properly, she will hopefully be more accustomed to human contact.'

'I have to say that, whatever else my brother was, he at least fed her for a while. She'll live then' It wasn't a question but the vet answered anyway. He looked at the dog's mournful eyes.

'I think so, with care. I would recommend leaving her here for more of your excellent nursing care, Miss Wykeham d'Evreux if that is alright with you?'

Elspeth nodded and smiled.

'Perhaps your niece can fetch some tablets from the surgery later this afternoon?'

'I'll get them' volunteered Luke 'I have to call at the hospital for a check-up anyway and then collect my gran's prescription and bring it back here.'

Tess smiled her thanks and bit her lip, maybe she had got this man wrong? The vet continued,

'And then in a day or two when she is stronger, I'd like to see her at the surgery for the day, to give her a full examination.'

Business concluded and tea drunk, the men prepared to depart.

'By the way,' Tess couldn't help asking, 'what type of dog is she?'

Elspeth chuckled at this and the vet confirmed her thoughts.

'Take your pick' he said, looking at the sorry stray lying there, one ear up and one ear down, and fur stuck out at every angle. 'A bit of this, a bit of that. Terrier is definitely involved somewhere, possibly Maltese terrier – but I wouldn't like to guess on the other parent.'

'Well that won't do' came Luke's voice. 'A Wykeham d'Evreux without a pedigree? The shame of it.'

Elspeth's eyes narrowed but her lips twitched.

'Are you making fun of my family name, young man?'

Tess turned to Luke.

'Don't do that for heaven's sake' she deadpanned 'I did that ten years ago and only just survived.'

Elspeth's eyes were crinkling with suppressed laughter.

Mr.Grafton departed and Luke went over to the dog, stroking her ears.

'You're no Hound of Hell are you?' he smiled, then he too said goodbye.

Tess went to see him out before she went upstairs to put on non-revealing and less embarrassing clothes. He turned at the door and handed her a hastily scribbled note, torn from the shopping-list pad on the kitchen dresser.

'You see' he winked,' I was telling the truth.'

Leaving her puzzled, he stepped out and closed the front door behind him. Tess unfolded the paper and read,

'*I thought you were a goddess.*
An angel on Earth, my fair maid.
Yet now I see, though still as fair,

You are, in fact, a mermaid.'

She chuckled despite herself, then flung the door open.

'That is truly awful' she shouted at his retreating back.

There was a burst of laughter as he turned and gave an exaggerated, courtly bow. She closed the door on him with a stupid grin on her face. She poked her head back in the kitchen and said she would go up and get changed, make breakfast for them, then take over while Elspeth had a rest.

'Thank you, my dear. I will take you up on that.' Her aunt's tone was much warmer, almost unrecognisable from the authoritarian voice that had first greeted her.

After breakfast, Tess gingerly lifted the little dog onto her knees, not knowing if she would accept it – but after a cursory glance up at her, she settled her head down and went to sleep.

'Will you keep her then? she asked her aunt.

'I most certainly will. Just let anyone try and take her away from me.'

Tess tried to dismiss the vision of her aunt, spear in hand, blue woad smeared on her face, taking on all comers.

'What will you call her?'

I've been thinking about that.' replied her aunt. 'When I was very young we had a dog, a

Sheltie. I wanted to name it but Hugo got his own way as usual, calling the name I chose a 'stupid name for a dog'. It ended up being Tess, which is why I preferred to call you Theresa.'

'Ah, I see now. A lifelong aversion to my name then?'

'It's grown on me. As have you.' Elspeth added and gave her a warm smile as Tess looked at her with surprise. Things were looking up. Elspeth opened the kitchen door.

'So, what was the name you wanted to call doggie-Tess? Are you going to give this dog the name instead?'

'I am. My chance to choose at last. I'm going to call her Tallulah.'

Tess blinked.

'It's a stupid name for a dog' she echoed.

'Don't care.'

Tess eyed the scruffy bundle of sticking-out fur.

'She's not a Tallulah, Elspeth.'

'Still don't care. She'll probably be known as Tally anyway' said Elspeth as she left the room.

'Thank goodness for that' murmured Tess.

'Don't push your luck.' Her aunt's voice drifted back from the hallway.

Ears like a bat, thought Tess.

Chapter 12

Tallulah, the small black dog of indeterminate breed, was having her day at the vet's today. Having been tended by two loving humans for a couple of days and looking much better for it, she was reluctant to make the journey to Whitby. This decision was taken out of doggy paws by the vet himself, who had picked up a poorly cat in the village and picked up Tally at the same time. If a dog can frown, then Tally frowned and gave them a 'how dare you abandon me?' look, then she seemed to realise who Mr. Grafton was and perked up a bit. With his promise to drop her back off late afternoon, that meant her humans now had a spare day.

'I think a visit to Darlington is in order' said Elspeth as Tess's life flashed before her at another 'torture by Porsche'.

'I'll drive' she offered, a little too brightly.

'I know the way so it makes sense for me to drive.' Elspeth replied.

'…but I haven't driven anywhere properly yet. The car needs a run…'

'I'm sure it will be fine' Elspeth said and then sighed. 'If I promise to drive slower, will that be alright?'

'What do you mean by slower?' asked Tess suspiciously. The details were very important in this case.

'At a speed that means your eyeballs remain in your head and don't pop out on stalks.'

'And then much slower than that?'

Elspeth adopted the expression of a child being told that she couldn't have any sweets.

'I *suppose* so. I didn't have you down as such a wimp.'

'If you had to drive with you, then you'd be a wimp too.'

'That doesn't make sense.'

'It does to me.'

Another sigh.

'I promise' said Elspeth, doing the Brownie salute.

And so it was that half an hour later, they found themselves on the road to Darlington. If it wasn't exactly a sedate pace then it was a definite improvement on her first experience. It was only when they were halfway there that Tess thought to ask why they were going.

'To have a word with Master Curwen's dancer girlfriend of course. Do keep up.'

'Didn't Luke say the alibi stood up?' asked Tess, not relishing a confrontation.

'Yes. It doesn't though, she was lying for him. Or has been tricked by him. Don't tell Luke though, it will stir things up in his mind again and it really doesn't matter-because Curwen didn't kill Hugo. No, I'm going to ask her about the ring. He may have given it to her or at least offered it to her.'

Tess swallowed hard before she said the next words, as though they might choke her.

'Didn't you... 'see' anything? Have you no idea where it is?'

Elspeth looked across at her and then back again when Tess pointed urgently in front of them.

'Stop panicking, I'm in control' she said, then 'No. I can't see the ring or sense it. It's in the nature of the ring that it has mystery surrounding it. I should perhaps see something if I had been wearing it recently but it has never been on my finger. Hugo took it just as soon as our mother died, which is why there is poetic justice ...' she stopped abruptly then started again.

'Hugo knew the Balefire ring was supposed to pass directly down through the female line, therefore it was mine by rights. He'd always coveted it. I'm sure that's why he's had such a miserable life and spent it feeling bitter about everything and everybody. Although he was always that way inclined. The ring can't reveal itself to me but I will find it.'

'Why Balefire?' asked Tess.

'Balefire is a fire in an open place, the same as a bonfire. The ring is supposedly a thousand years old and belonged to the Wykehams. The Weaver married one of them and told his stories round the fire, which was the same colour as the ruby in the ring. It has passed down through the Wykehams and it is our heritage Tess.'

Elspeth was very quiet for the rest of the journey, deep in thought. It was only later that Tess remembered the words '*our* heritage.'

Tess took in the countryside and the signpost directing you to Ormesby Hall and to Great Ayton 'the boyhood home of Captain Cook'. It was still stunning countryside but Tess found she was thinking of Weaver's Green and how beautiful she found it now. It was funny how much it had grown on her in such a short time.

On reaching the outskirts of Darlington, Elspeth pulled up outside an old brick building that looked like it had been a warehouse. On the wall outside the main door was a plaque announcing 'Natalia St. Clair' with quite a lot of letters after her name and proclaiming it to be a ballet school.

'I hate to say this but I thought she would be an exotic dancer, using snakes in inappropriate places. Or a lap dancer.' Tess admitted.

'That was my first thought too until I looked her up. More what I would have expected from that man.' Then Elspeth threw open the door.

Inside, the dance school had been fully modernised with wood, glass and mirrors everywhere. A couple of corridors led off the main reception area with arrows pointing to MAIN STUDIO and STUDIO 2. Elspeth marched up to a bored receptionist who was reading a glossy magazine.

'We're looking for Miss St. Clair' she said and the girl, not bothering to look up said 'Studio 2' with a vague arm wave to her right.

Elspeth grunted at her in reply then they walked in the direction of the studio. Behind a door marked '2', they could hear sounds of activity. The music which had drifted down the corridor had stopped. Tess was about to peer through the inner window to her left when the door opened and a thin, elegant woman with her dark hair in a chignon, appeared.

'*There* you are! she said in a disgruntled voice which had very faint traces of a foreign accent. 'You only have 15 minutes of the free half-hour taster session left – but you might as well come in as you've booked. You can still get a feel for it I suppose.'

She looked them up and down suspiciously then walked off in front of them as though she was on stage, beautifully erect and imperious.

'But…' began Tess.

The woman held her hand up to dismiss any further disruption of her time.

'Please stand there' said Miss St. Clair, indicating a place at the front.

'But…' Tess tried again.

'AND…' The ballet mistress nodded at a young girl in front of a machine and the music started again. Miss St. Clair started to wave her arms from side to side.

'Just follow me, I am a flower swaying in the breeze. Now a fairy dancing around the flowers.'

Tess's mouth formed the 'B…' again before she noticed that Elspeth was waving her arms too. Oh God, thought Tess before she too half-heartedly copied the dance teacher. At her side, unbelievably, her aunt was getting carried away, clod-hopping from foot to foot, trying unsuccessfully to copy the graceful movements in front of her.

Realisation came in a hot, embarrassed wave over Tess's skin when she watched Elspeth's 'dancing'. Elegant, erect and graceful in normal life, in attempting to dance, her aunt moved like an elephant with gout. Completely out of rhythm, she swayed one way as everyone else swayed the other. Every time she jumped from one foot to the other, the noise echoed and reverberated under the floorboards. The music thankfully came to an end, turned off by a now very amused assistant. Tess daren't look around her for reactions but could see through the long wall mirror that people were glancing at each other then lowering their eyes.

'That was good, everybody' intoned Natalia. 'Now we will try the running jump.'

Good? thought Tess. Miss St. Clair was either desperate for new blood or she was too busy looking at her own reflection in the mirror to notice she had an ugly duckling behind her. Or did she mean that Elspeth should take a running jump – preferably out of the door?

'Now watch closely. Four steps only, starting with your right foot and moving like an elegant swan in flight, elevate your right foot forward, your left pointed behind. At the same time, form a graceful movement with your arms, left above right and land as light as a feather from the swan. It sounds difficult yes?'

You've got it in one, thought Tess and turned to Elspeth for confirmation of this thought, only to see her taking it all in with a rapt expression on her face. Tess shut her eyes tightly for a second but when she opened them, they were still in the studio. It really wasn't just a bad dream.

Miss St. Clair demonstrated the movement most gracefully and it did indeed look easier when performed, rather than described.

Everyone took their turn individually, which was Tess's worst nightmare. Not so her aunt, who awaited her turn eagerly. There were varying degrees of success and a few thuds on landing.

'Remember' said Miss St. Clair, 'light as a feather.'

Too soon it was Elspeth's turn. Tess debated heading for the door or pretending to pass out but it was too late. Elspeth ran loudly and with great determination as though she was attempting to jump over a river in full flood. She took off, her legs in two directions, neither of them the right ones, whilst her arms were held out straight in front of her as though reaching to grasp a life-saving rope. Which she obviously missed as the next second, she landed with a thud that shook the studio. She then slid sideways for a few feet before ending up facing the wrong direction. This could only be called landing 'light as a feather' if the feather was still attached to an emu.

There was a silence. Tess risked a quick glimpse at the others' expressions, which ranged from those fighting not to laugh to those who were pretending it hadn't happened. Miss St. Clair was one of the latter.

'Yes…' she whispered with a glassy stare somewhere above Elspeth -the- dying -duck's head. Maybe she was contemplating being an accountant. She gave a visible shudder and came round. 'We'll just finish with a curtsey to the audience as – well, as elegantly as you can. Follow my movements.'

Her elaborate curtsey was attempted by Elspeth, who managed to hit her other, smaller, neighbour in the face as she flung her arms out to the side. Apologising profusely, she then waited until all the others had filed out before she went over to Natalia St. Clair who watched her approach warily.

'Did you enjoy it?' she asked Elspeth politely.

'Oh yes! I have always wanted to do ballet; I think I might join you and take it up.'

'R-really?' stuttered a wide-eyed Natalia.

'No, not really. You're quite safe, my dear.' And for the first time, Tess noticed a glint of mischief in her eyes, 'but perhaps you can help me on another matter?'

Natalia visibly relaxed and looked ready to agree to anything as long as Elspeth stayed away from her dance studio.

'Curwen Aberford' Elspeth said as Natalia pursed her lips.

'I don't want to talk about that man. I have seen the back of him, I hope. He just wanted my money and a place to stay. He didn't want me.' She stopped her tirade, suddenly looking wary 'I don't know where he is though and I'm not responsible for his debts, so I can't help you.'

'It's alright, we know he wasn't with you when you said he was. We're not going to tell the police.'

'I didn't lie. He was in my flat or so he told me. He was there when I left and the bed looked like it had been slept in when I got back. Only –,' she looked at the floor, 'I wasn't there for most of the time. We had an argument and I know I wouldn't have slept so I came to the studio to work on some difficult choreography and get him out of my system. When I returned, around 5.15a.m, he wasn't there. I don't know what time he left, only that he had been there at 9pm the previous evening and wasn't there on my return. I thought he must have gone early morning when he realised I wasn't coming back.'

'We know where he was and don't worry, he wasn't committing murder. He was where he is now, at Rook Hall in Weaver's Green, in case you need to know for any reason? He has committed another crime though, that of theft. He has taken a valuable ring of mine. Do you know anything about it?'

'He never gave me a ring although he had asked me to marry him that same night. I wouldn't, I know he has too many debts and would just keep sponging off me. I was getting sick of his lies. He said he would bring me a ring the next time he saw me and it would change my mind. He said it had a large ruby and other precious stones but I said I wouldn't change my mind, especially for an unlucky stone. That was the last I saw of him. I wanted him to go.'

Elspeth, after a moment's silence, merely said,

'Rubies have a bad press, they're not unlucky at all. In the right hands.'

'I wouldn't have wanted it anyway, whatever it was. Not from him – and it would have been stolen?'

'Yes, I'm afraid so. Well,' she looked across at Tess, 'A wild goose chase but I'm still determined to track it down.'

'We'll find it' said Tess, only now realising how important its recovery was to her as well.

'Good luck' Natalia St. Clair smiled 'and now I have my senior class if you'll excuse me?'

'Of course, thank you for your help.' Elspeth said as they began to walk down the corridor. The ballet mistress's voice followed them,

'And if you *do* want to take up dancing, there's another studio at the other side of town.' She winked as they both turned and laughed. Curwen really didn't deserve her, thought Tess.

Chapter 13

The sun shone down yet again on Weaver's Green the next day as if to make up for the apocalyptic storm of a few days before. Tess gazed around at the pretty village green, with houses dotted around its perimeter and mentally hugged herself. She had started to feel quite happy here, contrary to her expectations and even had a sense of belonging. She would have to leave and get a job soon but as her aunt seemed to have accepted her and wasn't in any hurry to kick her out, she would just enjoy her time here.

She had come out to pick up some milk and had left her aunt and Tally in the conservatory. Tally had passed her M.O.T. test with flying colours – a result of being a hardy cross-breed, the vet had said – and was now completing her recovery with the tender ministrations of her new best friend, Elspeth. Both were very happy about the situation.

Tess was just about to pop into the shop when, past the sheep wandering freely and past the ever-munching donkeys tethered on the green, she saw Berry. She was easily recognisable by the wild, curly mane of hair around her face and was sitting with someone at a table and chairs outside her cottage.

She walked over, stroking Clover and Daisy on the way and saw that the other person was George the gardener who was also Berry's next door neighbour.

'Come and join us' called Berry, dashing in for another cup. There were four chairs around the table and Tess sat in one of them. After Berry poured the tea out, Tess noticed there was an open notebook in front of them.

'Have I interrupted anything?' she asked.

'No, it's only a monthly meeting of the Weaver's Green allotment society' replied Berry.

'All two of you?' Tess couldn't help asking.

'There are eight of us altogether' Berry replied with a mock insulted expression on her face before laughing, 'but as hardly anything changes from month to month, the others have just left it to us to tell them if anything changes.'

'I thought there weren't any allotments here?' frowned Tess, vaguely remembering an earlier conversation.

'There aren't' replied Berry, ' but we live in hope.'

Tess looked perplexed. George explained, a wry smile on his face.

'We're an allotment society without allotments. That's why we've formed, to try and rent some spare land. The land in this vale is so fertile but all the good land has been built on over the years. The villagers who own these houses want to preserve their gardens for flowers and relaxation, not veg and hard work. I can see their point of view.'

George looked as though he could see anybody's point of view as he had a permanent smile and gentle eyes.

'You know why we can't have the field next to your 'cousin who isn't your cousin'' added Berry, 'so we're stuck because all the immediate surroundings are moorland and unsuitable for anything but sheep. There are a few areas of green 'over the top' but most are farms who either cultivate the land themselves or use them as campsites or caravan sites – or holiday cottages. We've just about run out of options. If we ask about land any further out, we'll nearly be at Whitby!'

'We can still do a bit in the back' said George stoically, nodding at their cottages.

'I can't, the donkeys will eat it all – and then try to eat what little veg plot they've left you George. I'm really sorry.'

'Nay lass, I'd rather see yon two happy than grow a garden full of potatoes.'

'I thought you were after Curwen's field for your donkeys though, not for allotments?' asked Tess.

'Have you seen it? It's plenty big enough for both. I can grow my flowers in my garden to sell– and then work on an allotment up there while I keep an eye on Clover and Daisy at the same time. It's a dream though' sighed Berry dejectedly.

'Well, if he sells it, maybe the next people would…' began Tess.

'He can't do that though' announced George and Tess saw from Berry's expression that it was news to her as well.

'What do you mean he can't do that?' asked Tess, her brows furrowed.

George immediately sat up straight.

'Ah, I might have spoken out of turn. If your aunt hasn't said anything, then don't mention it or I'll be in trouble. I just thought you would know.'

'That's that then' said Berry, 'the last hope is taken away now' and cast her eyes down.

There was a noise behind them and a small grey-haired lady came out of George's cottage, carrying a spare cup. George rushed up to take it off her hands as if it were an extremely heavy object and as she sat down, the newcomer asked with a smile,

'How is the Weaver's Green Donkey and Allotment society going then?'

Their glum upturned faces told her all she needed to know. She got up out of the chair.

'I know what you all need.'

Ten minutes later, they were all chattering over a fresh pot of tea and Olive's homemade coffee and walnut cake.

Olive was George's wife and was another lifelong resident. It turned out that Olive, Elspeth and Gwen had all gone to the village school together and were all still friends to this day. Olive had helped out at the reception desk in the Folklore Museum over lunchtimes to give Elspeth a break. She said she still missed it.

'Why did she give it up?' asked Tess, suddenly needing to know.

'That's something you will need to ask her Tess but I got the feeling she found it harder to cope on her own, the older she got. Don't mention that though, I don't think she likes to admit to any sort of weakness. And…well, she just seemed to lose heart. It had been coming on for a while, I think. '

The biggest surprise was that Luke was part of the allotment society. He seemed to have more invested in Weaver's Green than he did in Whitby, where he mostly lived and worked when he wasn't hobbling around in a plaster cast. He had found them a small patch of land on a smallholding just over four miles away but the owner had backed out, saying he realised he would need the land himself now his son was coming up to the age where he would be able to help him. Berry suspected the man's overbearing wife's influence but there was nothing they could do but accept it.

Jumping up suddenly. Tess remembered the milk she had been sent out to buy. Apologising, she excused herself and said that she would try to help in any way she could.

Bursting through the front door, she went straight into the kitchen, passing her aunt on the way out. 'I had my coffee black' came the accusing voice from the hallway.

Chapter 14

It was nearly midnight when Tess stopped trawling the internet for jobs in Norfolk. There was nothing she could find that didn't give her a sinking feeling in her stomach. She had to ask herself if she was just lazy or whether there was something else behind her lack of interest.

Why had she picked a degree in accountancy and finance to study anyway? She had wanted to do art but her father had asked her what she would do with it afterwards. She had to agree jobs would be few and far between and there would be plenty competition for them. At least this degree had kept her in full, well-paid employment. Until now.

She still had quite a lot of her redundancy money left as she hardly had to pay for a thing at Wykeham Grange. Her food was included in Elspeth's weekly order and her aunt wouldn't hear of her paying any board as Eustace had sent his daughter to her in a 'Mission of Mercy'. This last was said in deeply sarcastic tones as they both knew no such mission was needed. Still, she thought she ought to have a word with her aunt in the morning.

As she closed the door of her own sitting room and reached the staircase, she saw a light coming from Elspeth's sitting room – her inner sanctum. Tess had never set foot in there yet. She wondered if she should mention what was on her mind and once the idea took hold, it stayed there. No time like the present. She padded down the hall in her fluffy slippers and stopped outside the door.

'Elspeth, are you in there?' No answer. 'Sorry to bother you but have you got a minute?'

'Come in.'

This was unexpected. Tess had thought she would be sent away with a flea in her ear or at the very least, be confronted at the door by her aunt, accompanied by a belligerent expression.

She pushed open the door and took in the surroundings, which were not that much different to her own sitting room but bigger.

What caught her eye though was her aunt, seated at an armless fireside chair, leaning forwards towards a small occasional table in front of her. On the table was a large, shallow glass bowl, two feet wide at the rim. The green-yellow iridescence was bouncing off the glass with the aid of three flickering candles set around it. There was water in the bowl and pinpoints of light danced across the surface. Her aunt was staring intently into the bowl, almost in a trance.

Tess realised she had interrupted something she didn't understand and began to think she had dreamt the invitation to enter the room. All thoughts of her original question flown, she asked,

'What are you doing?' It seemed to be the only thing to ask, in the circumstances.

'Gazing into my crystal ball, what else?'

Just before Tess had time to wonder if this was supreme sarcasm, Elspeth looked up at her.

'Or in this case, crystal bowl.'

'Can you see anything?' Tess couldn't credit that she was asking this. If she had seen this when she first came here, she would have burst into derisory laughter. Now it seemed almost normal.

'I was just making sure, with good reason, that the vision I originally saw was the correct one. I don't normally resort to these confirmation tactics but I have to make sure that the vision which came unbidden to me without these aids, is correct. The stakes are too high and I need to be fair.'

'So, can you tell the future then?' asked Tess, hardly believing the words were coming out of her mouth.

'Not particularly the future. Sometimes it is but mostly in my case, it is the unknown past. I can't ask to be shown something, it comes spontaneously and occasionally unwanted. The scene is usually enacted in your mind but sometimes, it's just an unshakeable feeling. I think you experienced the same thing on the stormy night when we found Tallulah?'

She fixed Tess with a gimlet eye and Tess tried with all her might not to comprehend the meaning she knew was intended. Elspeth continued,

'This evening's vision has confirmed the truth of the first one, which I wrote down a while ago.'

Elspeth rose and pulled a sheet of paper from a drawer. Putting it into an envelope and sealing it, she handed it to Tess.

'Hide this somewhere in your rooms. Don't look at it till I tell you to. Now, what was it that you wanted?'

Tess took a few seconds to remember what had seemed so important ten minutes before.

'I was wondering – I have some money put by in the bank from my redundancy and,' she hesitated, not at all sure how this was going to be received, 'if I pay my way, would it be alright if I stick around here a while longer? Just until I get things straight in my mind. I know I was originally going to be here until you were well again and now I know you weren't ill in the first place; I don't know if...'

'Stop waffling girl!' came the school ma'am tones she knew and almost loved. Elspeth smiled a genuine smile and Tess relaxed.

'I think that is an excellent idea, barring the money situation. You may need that in the future so hold on to it for now. You are not costing me anything and your company is actually much appreciated. To my great surprise. So yes, welcome aboard!'

Tess grinned inanely and had this mad idea of rushing forward to hug her aunt but curbed it just in time and instead said,

'That's great Elspeth. I'm really enjoying your company too.' and meant it.

As she turned to leave, she noticed a sideboard behind the door, full of old framed photos on display. She glimpsed photos, or similar ones, that she had seen in her father's collection but what caught her eye was one of a young girl, obviously Elspeth. She had on a pale blue tutu and was striking a wonderful arabesque pose in front of a whole corps de ballet. Tess turned round in astonishment.

'You were a ballet dancer?'

'Only up to Grade 7. I was going to take it further but realised I didn't have that level of commitment

'But- Miss St. Clair's class. You were…'

'A clodhopper, yes.' She winked 'It's good to have a little fun sometimes, don't you think?'

Tess exploded with laughter and was still giggling to herself just before she dropped off into a deep sleep.

Chapter 15

Something had woken her and it was still pitch black outside. She rubbed her eyes and without putting a light on, opened her bedroom door and looked along the landing – nothing. Then she peered over the bannister, where she saw a dark figure standing on the stairs.

Schooled by now in expecting the unusual to happen, she managed not to scream this time, partly because the familiar figure had put a finger to her lips. Tess whispered

'What? Why?'

Elspeth heaved a sigh and put her hands on her hips in a 'How annoying' fashion, then whispered back to her through the wooden spindles.

'Get dressed, coat and shoes too, something dark. Don't make any noise or you'll wake the dog. Meet me outside.'

They stared at each other for a moment, wordlessly, then Elspeth made a shoo-ing motion with her hands so Tess went to get dressed. As she did so, obeying the command like a private on the parade ground, Tess wondered what it was this time. No dogs had been howling and it seemed a strange time for a brisk stroll round the green. She looked at her phone – 2.10 a.m. Closing the front door silently behind her, she tip-toed over to where Elspeth was standing against the side wall.

'Just follow me quietly and do as I do' ordered Elspeth.

'Your word is my command' whispered Tess.

'Shush' replied Elspeth.

They crept towards Rook Hall and into the driveway.

'Why are we here?' asked Tess.

'We're going to break in' answered Elspeth happily. 'if the spare key isn't where it used to be anyway.'

'But, Curwen?' gibbered Tess.

'Away. No car in the driveway, no lights on either when I walked round here earlier. He'll have found another girlfriend to support him. Now come on.'

They made their way round to the back and as they reached the porch, Elspeth reached down and moved, with difficulty, a large stone near the wall, coming up with a key in her hand.

'I knew Hugo kept a spare here, I haven't told Curwen yet.'

The door creaked as they opened it and then they were in a dark hallway. Luckily, Elspeth pulled her into a room immediately on their left and reaching into her pocket, pulled out a small torch. She went over to a desk under the window and started searching through the drawers.

'Now, in all the detective novels, there is always one drawer that is locked. Ah, here it is' and Elspeth bent down with a piece of metal fished out of a pocket and inserted it into the keyhole. A few seconds later, she pulled the drawer open.

Tess looked on, appalled. Picking locks? What sort of misspent youth had her aunt gone through?

'What are you looking for ?' she managed to ask.

'A receipt for the ring or any evidence of him selling it and to whom.'

'If he's away, why are we whispering?' asked Tess, whispering anyway.

'He has previous in these matters remember? He's not always where you think he is. Besides, he might come back.'

The search of the desk was fruitless and Elspeth continued the search of the ground floor with a nervous Tess acting as look out through the windows.

'Nothing' said Elspeth finally. 'Let's try his bedroom if we can find which one it is.'

'Why would he keep receipts there?'

'While we're here we might as well take a look' and Elspeth put her foot on the creaky stairs. Her brows knitted and she turned round.

'Watch out for the carpet at the top of the stairs' she said and then continued upwards, stopping outside the first door, where Tess caught her up.

There was a creak from the other side of the door. Tess stopped breathing and then saw the doorknob slowly begin to turn. Curwen's silhouetted figure appeared.

Tess screamed. Curwen screamed. Elspeth said 'For goodness sake.'

Putting his bedroom light on he stared at them both before pulling his dressing gown around him. He headed downstairs.

'Right, I'm sending for the police. Breaking and entering. And what have you stolen?'

His smiling, affable persona had disappeared and so had his previously cultured voice. His accent was harsher and more guttural. They followed him into a room on the ground floor, lit by a weak bulb hanging unshaded from the

121

ceiling. He held his phone, the blue light from it shining on his contorted face.

Elspeth sat on the uncomfortable settee and indicated Tess should too, then she addressed Curwen.

'Breaking and entering you say?' and held up the key. 'I'm afraid not. What have *we* stolen? I think the question is, what have *you* stolen, don't you? By all means, send for the police, it should be an interesting exercise. If you do, things will take a lot longer to clear up, to your own detriment. I think we can sort things out a lot easier between ourselves. Shall we try?'

Curwen looked angry, then unsure and finally crestfallen. He sat down heavily on a chair opposite them, his head in his hands. After a minute, he looked up at the silent, waiting figures.

'I didn't kill him!'

There was no response from the two women, although Tess's heart was pounding. He went on,

'The carpet at the top of the stairs is so worn and the bannister so rickety it moves around. It was just like the doctor said, he fell backwards down the stairs. His slipper was still caught in the big hole in the carpet, for god's sake.'

'Tell us exactly what happened and don't leave anything out' came Elspeth's calm and measured voice.

Curwen ran his hands through his hair, looking round him wildly. Then he began in a defeated voice,

'I tried to borrow some money from Nat, my girlfriend but she finished with me and went storming off. When she'd gone, I looked round the flat and found just over three hundred pounds but it wasn't enough. I still owed the casino seven hundred pounds and if I didn't pay it the next day – well, there are 'people' they hire to deal with non-payers. I just didn't have a penny; you've got to understand how I felt.'

'Oh spare me' said Elspeth's hard voice, 'if you didn't gamble it all away, you wouldn't have this problem. It's an addiction you're going to have to face up to, before it's too late. And stealing from your girlfriend? What a little worm you are. Continue.'

Curwen looked shocked but carried on anyway.

'I came here just before midnight, hoping the old man would be up and help me out. I just wanted him to give me some of my inheritance early. Just a few hundred pounds. An old miser like him wouldn't have missed it.

Of course, he said no. That's when he told me. He was only giving me the house under sufferance because of a promise he'd made to my aunt. He couldn't leave it to his sister either as you hated it. He said I certainly wouldn't be receiving any money from him as that was all going to you. Believe me, I felt like murdering him -but I didn't have the guts'

He looked at Elspeth.

'You know about the codicil in the will? He was going to leave you his house before you rejected it but instead, you get his money and I'm stuck with this.' He was like a petulant child.

'More than you deserve. You never saw your aunt for years before she died - or Hugo - but I don't blame you for that. Yes, I know about it. Are you ever going to finish this story?'

Curwen grunted.

'He told me to go. I started shouting at him, I didn't know what to do next. There was one ex-girlfriend I had left to try, then... Anyway, he went upstairs and I turned to go to the door. The next minute there was this thud. A series of thuds. I turned back and he was lying at the bottom of the stairs, his leg and his neck in weird positions and there was blood coming from his head. I knew he was dead but I also knew that I would get the blame if I was found here. I just wanted to get the hell out of there. Then I noticed his hand.'

'And the ring' breathed Elspeth.

'I thought I could sell it in the morning and pay off my debt, so I took it from his finger and got out as quick as I could, wiping both sides of the door handle as I went. I drove onto the moors and sat there until first light.

Through a contact, I found a man willing to buy it. He offered me five hundred pounds and I took it and paid the sharks off. I had to give the contact the hundred pounds I had left so I was still penniless but, after all, I was going to inherit the house…'

'Five hundred pounds? Do you know how much that ring is worth?' screeched Elspeth.

'Please don't tell me' he pleaded.

'Where is it now?'

'I honestly have no idea. He will have sold it obviously, for a lot more money than he gave me. I don't know who he was or the name of the contact. That's not how it works. I'm telling you the truth and I didn't kill the old man either!' Curwen finished; his eyes wild.

'I believe you' said Elspeth. 'You know about the codicil to the will now from the solicitor, I expect?'

Curwen laughed mirthlessly.

'The codicil. I can have the house to live in till I die and then it reverts to you or your relations. I can't sell the damn thing. I'm stuck in the house of horrors. The old sod had the last laugh. God, I hate it here.'

'I don't want you here in Weaver's Green any more than you want to be here. You sully the atmosphere even more than Hugo did. There may be a solution.'

Curwen sat straight and waited but Tess couldn't wait any longer.

'Why isn't your car in the driveway?' she asked.

He looked annoyed at the interruption.

'It was Nat's car. She found out where I was somehow and came to collect it this afternoon. Used her spare car key I suppose. She had her numbskull brother in tow. She didn't even knock at the door – just took it and by the time I saw her, their cars were disappearing through the gates.'

'How terribly unfriendly of her. No manners at all. The least she could have done was say hello' said Elspeth's heavily sarcastic voice.

It went over Curwen's head.

'A solution, you said?' he asked, leaning forward eagerly.

Chapter 16

Whitby was bathed in glorious sunshine which didn't do anything for the dark, vampiric image of the Goth festival which was taking place there. Tess felt there should be black, lowering clouds with the odd rumble of thunder.

All around her were people of all ages, dressed in beautiful Goth costumes with some Steampunk ones for added attraction. They must have taken many hours to make and attention to detail was striking.

There were vampires and vampiresses – with white faces, black smudged eyes, red lipstick and the occasional trickle of (hopefully fake) blood running from their lips. There were Victorian gentlemen who could pass for Sherlock Holmes, a few decaying brides whom Tess wasn't sure were Brides of Dracula or Miss Havisham. There was a very authentic Captain Jack Sparrow complete with female pirate and there were representations of the undead – male and female.

There was even a huge Chewbacca from Star Wars, guarded by Stormtroopers. The younger children loved them even if most of them had no idea who they were. You could see all the parents explaining to them. Nobody seemed to mind that they weren't exactly Goths as the whole festival had a friendly, laid-back vibe.

After an hour wandering around amongst the Goths, Tess found a little café at the bottom of the famous 199 steps leading up to St. Mary's Church and Whitby Abbey, and sat outside, watching the slightly surreal world go by.

They had left Tally with Gwen, who was one of her favourite people, along with Luke. Tess had been allowed to drive here as they had to bring Curwen with them and Elspeth's was only a two-seater. There wasn't a lot of room in Tess's car either and Curwen, though not being the tallest of people, looked very squashed and uncomfortable in the back. The discomfort though was at least partly due to Elspeth's presence and the fact that all his attempts at conversation had been met with a wall of silence.

Elspeth and Curwen were now at the family solicitors and had been for nearly two hours. Tess was meeting her aunt outside the station where she was buying Curwen a one-way ticket to an undisclosed destination with the promise never to darken her village again.

She looked at her watch and wandered slowly to their rendezvous. She couldn't see her anywhere so strolled a little further on towards the harbour. A group of people with green faces and dressed in green rags, danced a wild, whirling dance, aggressively shouting at each other and banging their wooden staffs on the ground in a ritual. From further down, she could hear sea shanties battling with fantasy bard music.

When the performance was done, she turned back towards the station and was arrested by the sight of Elspeth, standing on the harbourside next to a Pirate ship, in earnest conversation with Dracula and his bride. As Tess wondered whether or not to interrupt, she saw the Goths hand her a business card and they all shook hands. Was Elspeth a closet Goth? Tess smiled until she realised that Elspeth's love of folklore would mean she was quite at home here.

'Fish and chips.' Elspeth's voice floated towards her making itself heard above the din. 'We can't come here and not have them, although there is a queue that may mean we'd get them at suppertime.'

'I know that's supposed to be the best place – as is obvious by the queue – but isn't there anywhere else we could go? I'm starving' whined Tess.

Elspeth merely looked amused and pointed up at a tall, red-brick building.

'The restaurant above that pub serves them and has wonderful views over the harbour.'

'That'll do then.'

*

After the meal, Tess tentatively asked how it had gone at the solicitor's but was met with a 'Later'. Tess was so full she could hardly move so when Elspeth suggested climbing the 199 steps to get the best view of Whitby, she groaned.

'Can we come back and do that another time *before* we eat?'

Elspeth laughed and agreed.

'Well is there anything you would like to do then before we set off back? There's a café called Sherlock's on Flowergate with lovely cake?'

Immediately she said this, Tess stopped in her tracks, as she had another flash of the scene that had bothered her since she woke this morning from something she thought was a dream.

'What? What is it?' asked Elspeth, looking interested rather than worried.

'Nothing, I just thought perhaps we could just wander round the Old Town instead for half an hour and you could tell me a bit about it?'

'I used to come to schools here or to the shops and cafes, for fish and chips and the occasional ice cream I know a little about the history of the Old Town, I'm sure there will be a guide you can buy though?'

'No, just want to walk off this meal I think?' Tess smiled.

They wandered round the winding, narrow streets that climbed up the hill. They looked at jet jewellery shops and hand-made soaps. There were rock shops, book shops, toy shops and antique shops. They stopped at a popular bakery to buy some of their famous lemon buns, to take home for tea.

All the while, Tess was not her normal chatty self and Elspeth kept darting sidelong glances at her. Tess stopped walking.

'What's up there?' she asked, pointing at yet another winding, cobbled street with shops disappearing round the bend.

'I've no idea' her aunt answered, staring at her strangely, 'I don't recognise the street. Shall we have a look?'

'Yes' said Tess automatically, her eyes on a little alleyway leading off from the top bend. 'There should be a little…'

She hardly dare voice what should be there but the next minute, she found herself standing in front of the same jeweller's shop that had kept filling her mind. The shabby paintwork was in dark blue with gold lettering proclaiming PENMAN'S Fine Jewellery. There were bull's eye windows in the small panes that made up the Victorian bow-fronted window.

'You 'saw' this didn't you?' Elspeth sounded excited.

'I, yes, it's just been flashing into my mind ever since I woke. I can't understand'

'Possibly, because I should have had the ring after my mother died and didn't, it was blocked from my sight – but will have guided you to it as you are one person removed from its destiny. Through you, it's revealing itself.'

'How can I have seen a shop, in a street I don't know, in a town I last visited when I was four, maybe five?

'Welcome to my world' smiled Elspeth in answer and opened the door, making the shop bell above it clang noisily.

'I hope the ring is there after all this' Tess scowled and Elspeth stood back again.

'Lukas is in Whitby today. Here is his number' she fished in her pocket and tore a sheet out of a notebook. 'Ring him and tell him to get straight round here in an official capacity as there might be problems. Wait out here for him unless I call you' and with that, she left Tess staring after her, on the pavement outside.

A few minutes later, a police car came tearing down the hill. The uniformed driver stayed in the car as Luke leapt out and grabbed hold of her shoulders.

'What's wrong? Are you alright?' Tess looked worried as she nodded. He had said he wasn't far away so to hang on and then he rang off before she could explain more. It seemed enough that she might be in trouble and she had called him. She felt a little guilty and a little pleased at the same time.

'Is it Elspeth? ' he said, looking puzzled and when he got a mumbled response he added 'It's not my gran is it?'

'Oh god, I'm so sorry to inconvenience you. My aunt made me call you. She's in there, trying to get her ring back.'

'Ah, the famous ring' he said and his shoulders relaxed. He opened the door and the bell announced their entry.

'Hello, Detective Sergeant Mills. How nice to see you. This – person – says he's never had a ring in his shop of the description I gave him. He's lying.'

'You're sure of your facts Miss Wykeham d'Evreux?' Luke said, showing his badge to the man and playing along. He looked surprised as Elspeth replied.

'Absolutely sure. Tess told me. She saw that it was here.' She put invisible quotation marks around the 'saw'.

Tess wanted to sink through the floor and she blushed as Luke slowly turned to face her, his eyebrows raised.

'I have been trying to assure madam that such an object has never been in my possession. A large, medieval Blood ruby, surrounded by tiny pearls and emeralds in a solid gold setting? I'm hardly going to forget it, am I officer?' Penman laughed obsequiously and unconvincingly.

'Its very age and rarity are very good reasons to keep quiet about it though, wouldn't you say?' replied Luke.

' I can only reiterate – as I keep telling madam – I haven't got it and have never had it.'

A calm came over Tess and she stared into the odious little man's eyes.

'That's not true, is it?' she smiled as he drew back, thrown off balance for the first time at the certainty in her voice. 'You do have it here on these premises at this very moment. I suggest you go into the back rooms, go to the set of drawers on your left and bring it to us from where you've been hiding it, before I ask this nice policeman to arrest you'

'For w-what? he stammered.

'On suspicion of knowingly handling stolen goods and obstructing the police for starters' said Luke 'and if I have to get a warrant to search these premises, you're in serious trouble.'

Penman's piggy eyes had gone the widest they could behind his spectacles. He stood, still and silent, unable to tear his eyes away from Tess. He eventually moved in a stilted fashion, walking to a door leading to what looked like a workshop and there was a wait of a few minutes. Just when Luke was getting ready to follow him in case he'd made a break for it, he shuffled back through.

'Could this be it?' he whined faux-innocently 'I didn't recognise it from the description the lady gave. It's too dull for a ruby, I thought it was just a faded glass stone set in tarnished brass…'

'Then you're definitely in the wrong business aren't you?' said Elspeth. 'Have you ever thought of opening a soap shop instead?'

135

The man stuck his head down. They all looked at the box he held in which the ring was displayed. The stone was rather dull and the gold didn't shine but even to Tess's inexperienced eyes, it looked an expensive piece.

'Well, surprise, surprise' said Elspeth. 'I'd say that was it, wouldn't you? Luke, are you going to arrest him now?'

'Please, no. I bought it in good faith –' Ironic laughs greeted this statement. 'If I'd realised it was the ring you were telling me about, well of course I…' he trailed off.

'That's up to you' Luke said, answering Elspeth's question.

'Let the weasel go' said Elspeth dismissively, grabbing the ring, 'I've got what I came for.'

You're lucky this time' scowled Luke at Penman, who was almost in tears of self-pity, 'but I'm keeping my eye on you from hereon in. One wrong move and you won't know what's hit you.'

To the sound of sniffling gratitude, all three of them went out of the shop, slamming the door behind them and nearly making the bell fall off. Luke looked questioningly at them, his hands on his hips.

'Well?' he asked.

'I knew we'd have trouble. He wasn't going to admit it and just hand it to me because it *was* stolen. I knew it was there because Tess had 'seen' this shop and I trust her implicitly.'

After thanking Luke, she marched back off down the hill. The police car was still there, its driver looking on bemused. He'd probably been expecting an armed robbery at the very least.

'And you' said Luke, placing his finger gently on the tip of Tess's nose, 'are turning into your aunt.'

'God forbid' said Tess as she went to join her aunt and pretended she didn't know his real meaning.

*

By the time Tess arrived at the car park, Elspeth was standing at the quayside, chatting to someone. Some more Goths, or were they the same? There were a lot of vampires around. She saw Tess and mimed 'Five minutes' holding her fingers up. It had been a full day so Tess went back to her car, sitting in the driver's seat to close her eyes for a couple of minutes.

On opening them, she saw her aunt walking in her direction. She sat up and started to put her seat belt on when, to her horror, Elspeth got into the car two places in front of her, closed the door and pulled her seat belt on. She sat there quietly, facing forward as Tess got out of her own car door.

As she did so, she saw an irate elderly man, red-faced and parking ticket in hand, walk very quickly towards what was obviously his car. He reached the car before Tess and pulled the driver's side open, leaning in.

'What the hell do you think you're doing?' he shouted. 'Get out of my car or I'll call the police!'

Tess had a two-second thought about Luke turning up again which was enough to galvanise her into action as Elspeth mumbled something about all these cars looking the same.

'I'm terribly sorry sir, she can't help it. I'm her nurse. Your car is the same colour as mine' she indicated her car further back. 'She's just forgetful that's all. Many apologies. Come along dear.'

Oh boy was she going to suffer for this later.

By this time, Elspeth had got out of the car without another word and they both got into Tess's car. There was silence. Tess waited for the tongue-lashing as she watched the man, still grumbling, lock his car and give Elspeth a suspicious look before he went off. There were a few seconds of quiet then,

'Dear?'

Tess fumbled with her seatbelt, her mouth twitching.

'My nurse?'

More silence – then they both turned to look at each other and spontaneously burst into laughter. With Tess, it was mostly relief but Elspeth seemed to be really tickled by the charade and was now wiping tears from her eyes.

'I'd like to assure you' she managed eventually 'that I am not going senile. I have a lot on my mind at the moment and was deep in thought. Honestly.'

Tess told her that she was the most competent person she knew and they were the same type of car which she wasn't even used to seeing anyway. She started the car as Elspeth brought out the box with the ring in it.

'It *is* the right one isn't it?' asked Tess, looking at the dull and unremarkable object, 'Only I was expecting something more spectacular.'

In answer, Elspeth took the ring and placed it on the middle finger of her right hand. The transformation was immediate. The gold shone, the pearls and emeralds glinted and the ruby glowed like the setting sun.

'More like that?' whispered Elspeth, obviously in awe herself.

Tess gasped and laughed with amazement, while the true owner of the ring sat admiring her birthright with a beatific smile on her face.

Chapter 17

Breakfast overlooking the moors and vales was something Tess would miss when she eventually found a job and had to leave. She had settled into this life and this village incredibly well, considering she had been dreading the whole visit. They had been watching Tally running round in circles outside in the garden with George breaking off to throw a ball for her every couple of minutes. Panting, she had come in for a drink of water and was now settled across Elspeth's feet, head on paws. Tess glanced across the table to check her aunt's ring was on her finger. It was. Elspeth caught her eye.

'I don't think I'll ever let it out of my sight now' she smiled. 'It was always meant to come to me, handed down through generations of Wykeham women and I feel it brings me closer to my ancestors. I could never forgive Hugo for keeping it. The Balefire ring is where it should be now.'

'It was obvious the ring belonged to you, it came to life when you put it on, if you can say that about an inanimate object.' said Tess.

'I do think it has a 'life' of its own and I feel like I've got my own life back now. I feel energised and I have got my confidence back.'

'I haven't noticed a lack of confidence in you before Elspeth. No one would ever accuse you of being a shrinking violet' laughed Tess.

'Not in my manner particularly,' Elspeth agreed 'but in doing things. It even got so I let the folklore museum go into decline because I didn't have enough faith in people wanting to see it. According to the Goths though, they do.'

'Ah, is that why you were talking to the Goths then?'

Elspeth looked up sharply at Tess then smiled enigmatically.

'Perhaps' she said. 'I also stopped telling stories to visitors and the local children – and to other schools in the area. I miss that more than anything. Storytelling is in our blood.'

She nodded at Tess to include her in this and Tess didn't tell her that she even had difficulty with writing 'What I did in the holidays' at school. Elspeth was on a high so she kept quiet.

'You can open the envelope I gave you now, by the way.'

'I've already opened it.'

Elspeth stopped, her cup halfway to her lips.

'Do you ever do as you're told?'

'When there's good reason. I didn't open it until after we came back from Rook Hall though'

'And?'

'You saw and wrote exactly what he described. And yes, I'll admit that was spooky.'

Elspeth looked satisfied and put the last piece of toasted teacake in her mouth, then sat back, watching Tess drink her coffee. This unnerved Tess, who was wondering what she had done wrong.

'What?' she asked with suspicion.

'Don't you want to know what happened at the solicitor's?' asked her aunt.

Of course she did but she daren't ask. If it was good news – fine. If not, she didn't want to be on the receiving end of her ire.

'I just figured you'd tell me when you were ready, besides, events with the ring overtook that particular visit.'

Elspeth glanced at the ring and then said,

'If you've got time, I'll tell you.'

'Of course I have, what else would I be doing?'

Elspeth began.

'The codicil that prevented Curwen from ever selling Rook Hall or even renting it out, was absolutely legal and there was no way he could get out of it. Except that I had been on the phone to Mr. Ericson, our family solicitor, first thing in the morning so by the time we got there, it had been mostly drawn up.'

'What had?'

'Don't interrupt.'

'Yes ma'am, sorry ma'am.'

'Curwen was to sign the Hall over to me. As it was going to come to me anyway in the unlikely event of me outliving him, it was relatively easy. You were there at the Hall when we discussed a possible solution if we visited the solicitors – well, this was the outcome. The solicitor and I 'suggested' that I pay him half of the market value, it being valued as a 'do-er upper' rather than a ready-to-move into house. The ungrateful chancer wanted more. I told him he was lucky I was offering anything as I had to use my inheritance. He could take it or leave it. He took it.

The conditions to our contract were that if he ever came to Weaver's Green again or contacted me or my family, he had to forfeit the money.'

'Conditions, you said. What were the others?' interrupted Tess at her peril.

'Just one – that he attend a Gamblers Anonymous residential course, which I set up for him. It's in the middle of nowhere, without internet and they are not allowed their phones. If he attends the full eight-week course, bed and board paid for, then he receives the money.'

'That is such a great idea Elspeth' said Tess in surprise, 'and so good of you to have his welfare at heart.'

'Don't know about that, can't abide the man but it is an addiction and I don't like to see anyone struggling.'

Tess smiled warmly at her aunt.

'Do you think it will do any good in the end?' she asked.

'It has two chances so I hope he makes the most of it.'

Tess thought about it for a minute then pulled a face.

'Do you really think you can sell Rook Hall? It's very, well, haunted-looking, I suppose. It has a bad feel about it. You must feel it too?'

'On the contrary, the bad feeling went when Hugo died. He was the cause of it, not the house. You're just getting the negative vibrations from it all. Some people like these old Gothic-style houses. They have character at least.'

Elspeth stopped and smiled the particularly smug smile that infuriated Tess.

'What now?' asked Tess.

'You mentioned the Goths?'

'Ah yes, I suppose they like that type of thing – obviously' smiled Tess

'The couple I met yesterday knew the house and remembered me from when the village used to celebrate Halloween. They love the house and can envisage it all done out in an original Victorian style – which they wouldn't have to change much – and will possibly open it as a Gothic Experience guesthouse, they haven't decided yet. It's perfect for them, close to Whitby for the festivals but also in the village that has been called the Birthplace of North Yorkshire Folklore. Weaver's Green is full of old myths and legends and is the home of the Wykeham Witches.'

'So are they interested?'

'They are coming to have a look at it before they go back to Wakefield. They've asked for first refusal. It might not even make the estate agent's books at this rate.'

'That is unbelievable. They must be quite mad but…'

Tess stopped mid-sentence as two words filtered down into her brain.

'Wykeham Witches? Wykeham as in our family name? Witches?' her mouth fell open as Elspeth smiled then replied.

'Seers and healers, is what they were. Not witches. Not in the culturally stereotyped meaning of the word anyway. Some people have gifts which people don't understand, even today, so you can imagine what it was like hundreds of years ago. I will tell you their story one day. It is in the book.' Elspeth looked directly into the Wykeham eyes of Tess, 'We've always carried the name proudly, throughout the generations.'

Tess took a few moments to process this. Correction, this would take years to process properly. Was there really something in all this 'seeing' and 'feeling' malarkey that loomed large in her life at Weaver's Green?

'Now' said Elspeth, dismissing the subject, there are a few more things you need to know before you go and see your friend Berry.'

147

Chapter 18

Earlier, Tess had asked her aunt for Berry's phone number. She rang and asked her to get the Weaver's Green (Donkey and) Allotment Society together in an hour – or as many as she could anyway. Now she was making her way over to Berry's cottage, dragging Tally with her. She was unable to sit still for a moment longer, it was like she was sitting on a wasp's nest. She was so eager to get there that they had to call her twice before she heard them and saw a sea of arms waving at her from outside the pub. She ran over.

They had pulled two picnic tables together, overlooking the rowan trees and the expanse of grass on the green. The donkeys were tethered a little further along to the right. As everyone moved up for Tess to sit down, she noticed there were a couple of strangers there.

There was Berry opposite, then George and Olive, then Gwen – who as far as she was aware only wanted to eat Luke's allotment produce, not tend to it. Then on this side there was – she leaned forward – Oh, the man himself. Luke gave her a heart-melting smile which she half-returned. Tally ran straight up to him, and jumped onto his knee, showing herself to be a shameless hussy flattered by good looks and compliments. Tess watched the little dog with her head against his, love shining out of her eyes. She would have to have a quiet word with her when she got her home. Then Tally jumped down to have a drink out of the water bowl, jumping back up to put her soaking wet whiskers against Luke's face for another kiss.

'Eurgh! Get off!' he yelled in mock indignation so Tally went round the other side to see her friends and get the lead twisted around their legs. They were trying to extricate themselves while everyone laughed, so Tess took the time to have a quick look at the other two people between her and Luke. There was a middle-aged man with a weather-beaten face which had seen a lot of the great outdoors. He wore a mild expression and an open-necked shirt with the sleeves rolled up to the elbows. He nodded and smiled at her.

Next to Tess sat a lady, perhaps in her 60s – it was hard to say. Her hair was short, spiky and dyed blonde. She wore round purple-rimmed spectacles and an outsize pair of bib and brace overalls. She too, smiled at Tess. Berry began to speak.

'This is Tess, who has called us all together on some secret mission that we must never disclose, even when they torture us.'

Tess rolled her eyes but laughed anyway.

'And Tess, this is Steven and this is Charmian, usually just known as Shah. You know the others.'

'Hello everyone. For your first mission, you must infiltrate the Whitby and District Allotment Society and report back... Actually, it was Aunt Elspeth who sent me here and I have important but not secret news to tell you.'

Tess stood up at the end of the tables with her back to the green, so that everyone could see her, then she began to tell them the whole story. That Elspeth had bought the house from Curwen for a good price. He hated the house; it was just the money he wanted. That she had high hopes of selling it to a Goth couple who were coming to view it and were very keen. That she was selling the house and garden separately to the old Folklore museum barn and the field at the side. That she was keeping the barn and land immediately surrounding it including the car park and frontage but was going to give the field behind, stretching right up to the treeline and the moorland beyond, to the allotment society to share out and the other part for use as grazing for the donkeys.

There was a pause and then loud cheering broke out and lots of hugging took place, mostly involving Tess. Tally looked a bit miffed at not being the centre of attention so everyone made a fuss of her. Tess watched her lap it up and couldn't even recognise the little creature from that first night, unresponsive in Elspeth's arms.

Tess looked up amongst all the chaos and saw Luke slip silently into the pub. She was disappointed he didn't want to discuss it but it was up to him. It probably wasn't as important to him as it was to Berry anyway. She needed to ask the others something.

'Elspeth asked me to take you up to the field to scc if it fits the purpose well enough. Would you all be able to come now? I've got the key for the farm gate across the bottom. Apparently, Hugo thought you might take the donkeys there against his will, Berry, so he had the padlock put on.'

Tess shook her head in disgust at this but Berry looked guilty.

'I'm afraid I did try; I didn't think he'd notice them for an hour first thing on a morning but he'd locked it by then. Now they have a home at last.'

'And apparently' Tess went on, 'as the land was originally used as agricultural land as part of the original Weaver's Farm, there will be no need to apply for change of use. The growing of produce, the erection of tool storage facilities and grazing land are all included. Berry, you are allowed to put some sort of covered shelter up for Clover and Daisy, to keep them warm and dry.'

'Oh it just gets better!' shouted Berry, nearly deafening George, 'I can't thank you and Miss Wykeham d'Evreux enough.'

'I didn't do anything; she had already decided what to do but I wholeheartedly agree with it.'

'Can we take the 'girls' up with us to see their new home now?' asked Berry.

'Of course, I don't see why not.'

A voice came from the pub doorway.

'Before you do, perhaps we could celebrate this occasion in the correct manner?' and Luke held up two bottles of champagne, dripping with condensation.

'Hurray!' everybody shouted in a passable imitation of the Famous Five, and grabbed a glass as Des came round with a tray. Des smiled at Berry and gave her a hug while Gwen and Olive exchanged knowing looks.

'I wanted to bring the ice buckets too but Luke said that it wouldn't be around long enough for that.' laughed Des.

'Too right' said Berry and Shah in unison then grinned at the telepathy and clinked their glasses together.

Luke came round to Tess's side to pour her champagne. Then crouched down next to her.

'Well done. Told you there was more to Elspeth than the Miss Trunchbull effect didn't I?'

'I'm just coming to realise that' replied Tess truthfully, 'and remind me to tell you about the ballet dancing lesson sometime.'

You could see the letters of 'ballet dancing' forming a big question mark above his head, by the expression on his face.

'Anyway' she continued, 'you shouldn't be spending your money on champagne. Not that I'm complaining.'

'It's a double celebration I suppose. I've been working the odd day but I'm back at work full time on Monday so I want to make the most of my last weekend of freedom.'

'Oh, we won't be seeing you around as much then?' She tried to keep the disappointment out of her voice, 'and what about the allotment?'

'I do have days off you know, this isn't the London Met. Besides, whatever days I do the allotment, I'll probably stay with Gran for the night. She said she enjoyed my company while I was recovering and I enjoyed hers too. The flat is cold, bare and impersonal.' He then brought his focus back. 'So I'll probably still see you around then?'

He formed it as a question but Tess found she didn't know in which tone to answer it. He couldn't have meant anything other than a throwaway remark.

'Of course' she settled for and drank most of her champagne down in one go, making her eyes water.

*

They must have looked a strange parade for any casual observers. Eight assorted people, two donkeys and a ball of black fluff called Tally. They went up the compacted earth driveway at the side of the barn to reach the field. While Luke and George struggled to get the padlock to open, Tess looked back at the old car park to their right and the Folklore Museum beyond it towards the road. Olive followed her gaze.

154

'What's Elspeth doing with the old barn, did she tell you?' she asked.

'No, nothing. She was just full of plans for this field and just wanted me to tell you all as soon as possible. I know she's keeping it, possibly until she decides what to do? I don't know, has she said anything to you Gwen?'

'Not really' Gwen shook her head. 'I know she's very fond of the old place though.'

There was a cheer from Berry as the gate opened and they all trooped in, sizing it up by eye and treading the long grass down. Berry took the halters off the donkeys and they immediately put their heads down to eat.

'Will they be alright?' asked Tess, scanning the boundaries. 'I haven't checked if everything is secure.'

She wasn't sure about letting Tally off the lead in case there were holes in the hedges she could get through to make a dash for the moors. Although, she had stayed round here before they found her and she didn't think the little dog would stray far from her happy home now.

'If there's grass to eat, they'll be alright.' Berry laughed, then looked across at the boundary hedge at the far side. 'That would be a good place to put their shelter as it's sheltered already to an extent.'

Turning to the others who were in rapt discussions about the land, she interrupted.

'I know it's a bit further to go if we have the allotments at the far end of the field but would anybody mind if I have Clover and Daisy at this end? It's nearer for me to come at least twice a day to see to them but also they will see everyone pass by and they love human interaction and being petted.'

'We were just talking about that' replied George. 'This end of the field slopes very gently down to the barn and the road but the top end looks as though it evens out into flat land. So that solution sounds best for us all.'

Everyone grinned and looked pleased with themselves. They had been waiting a long time for this.

'We'll need water,' said Shah, 'is it laid on near here?'

'I'm sure Elspeth had water in the museum, didn't she gran?' asked Luke.

'Yes, two toilets with sinks at the back and a storeroom next to it that had a large sink too' Gwen replied.

'We used to make our cuppas there.' Olive added.

'We could perhaps run the water up to the border between the donkey field and allotments, with a stop tap, so none of us has that far to go?' said Berry.

'If you do want sheds on your plots' chimed in Tess,' you'll probably need some sort of track extending from the driveway to the top of the field for vehicles to take heavy things up?'

Steven, who had been mostly quiet up to then said,

'I've got a mate who can put some building rubble down this side, just so it's not muddy in winter and gives us a bit of purchase on the soil?'

'And I can get a fence put alongside it so my girls are closed off from it.' added Berry.

'How much land will you need for them Berry?' someone asked and there followed much discussion about size of different areas, drainage, multi sheds or one communal larger shed, access etc. that lasted well over an hour. At the end of that time, they concluded that there was plenty room for the donkeys and 8 good size allotments with the track running at the bottom of them all. That was for the five owners who were here and the three who were absent today. In addition, there would be plenty spare land left at the top, leading up to the tree line. They would advertise locally as the space could easily be divided up into another six medium-sized allotments if there was any interest.

'Now the hard work begins' said George but they all looked incredibly happy at the thought of all this hard work. Tess could imagine them going home now, their heads full of plans.

They all came and gave her a hug on their way out and she got a nuzzle from Clover and Daisy too. Berry was taking them back to the green so they didn't gorge themselves all at once on the fresh long grass.

There was just Luke left and he held his arms open, walking towards her. She didn't know what her expression must have been like but on seeing it he did a comedy jump back and a fake flinch.

She laughed at this and the next second she was enveloped in his warm, strong arms, his cheek, smelling of sandalwood, next to hers. He released her and after setting the padlock and giving her the key, he walked off in the opposite direction with a smile and a wave. He was only giving her a friendly hug just like everyone else had, so why did it feel so much more special?

Chapter 19

Tally's little legs spun round like Catherine Wheels as she trotted along towards the parade of shops. She had been on a long walk on the moors with the younger of her humans and had tired her out. Tess's tongue was hanging out further than Tally's.

As they passed the tea rooms, she glanced in the window and saw the three witches from Macbeth huddled over a cauldron. She would have to put a stop to this vivid imagination that had overtaken her recently, she thought with a grin. Deep breath – and saw her aunt, Gwen and Olive huddled over a pot of tea. They looked up and waved, beckoning her in. She pointed at Tally and in answer, Sally, the owner came out.

'Bring her in, she'll sit under your table and I'll bring her a bowl of water and an extra teacup for you.'

That sounded good to Tess who was gagging for a cuppa. Inside, she noticed four pieces of cake on a plate. Had her aunt known she would pass by?

'You'd better bring another piece of coffee fudge cake too Sally.' Elspeth shouted over to her.

'Is someone else joining us?' asked Tess, puzzled.

'No, we need a piece for the Pixies' luck.' explained Gwen, although it didn't seem much of an explanation.

'Of course you do' mumbled Tess as she sat in the spare chair.

'Don't mock it, you should know us by now. If you buy or bring a piece of cake for the Pixies they will bring you luck in your immediate future and your recent endeavours. You'll have to read the story in my book. This is to make sure the house sale goes smoothly.' Elspeth told her.

Tess raised her eyes to heaven but then dived forwards with the others for a piece of cake, leaving the fifth piece, which Sally had just brought, on the plate for the Pixies. For heaven's sake, thought Tess, although the Pixies had a treat awaiting them, the cake was delicious.

'I had a pixie doll when I was young.' Tess said through a mouthful of cake, 'I called her Pixie Jayne Tiny Willoughby.'

Three faces turned towards her and didn't say a word.

'In my defence' she bristled, 'I was only four.'

They turned back, accepting this.

'So, are you celebrating then?' Tess asked, mindful of the house viewing with the Goths this morning.

'We are' replied Elspeth 'bearing in mind that there is nothing drawn up yet, hence the Pixie cake. They seem desperate to buy though and I did give them a good price. They said they have wanted it for the last seven years, since they first set eyes on it.

'That is such good news' grinned Tess.

'There's no accounting for taste' muttered Olive. 'I've been asking what on earth they're going to do with it' She was unable to believe somebody actually wanted to live in that dark, forbidding old house.

'It's a substantial house' added Gwen 'but it's not everyone that would want to take it on, so you were lucky there Else.'

Else? thought Tess. No, sorry, that was a step too far for her . She'd come from Great Aunt to Elspeth and that was far enough.

'Actually' Elspeth jumped in 'he is a builder as well as a Goth and he gave it a thorough going over. Apparently it is structurally sound with very little repair work needed. Well built in the first place, he said. The décor would mostly have been fine too but quite a lot of it is tired and worn and needs replacing or a lick of paint. They are keeping all the old original features, thank goodness. By the way, it's about time we stopped calling them the Goths and started calling them Kevin and Sharon.'

'You're joking! laughed Tess 'I expected Morticia and Gomez at least.'

She stopped laughing when Elspeth held her hand up in warning.

'Kevin and Sharon Brown, from Wakefield and hopefully new residents of Weaver's Green. They are really nice people, salt of the earth. They grow their own veg and will use their own garden for it but are very pleased about the allotments being next to them. They are looking forward to exchanging tips and seeds. The donkeys – they said that their children would love them and if Berry needed a hand, she would have two very willing small helpers.'

'They do seem good people and I have learnt today's lesson - 'Don't judge a book by its

162

cover' said Tess, suitably chastened and not for the first time.

'Haven't we all?' said Gwen and Olive nodded her agreement. 'We'll make them all very welcome at Weaver's Green.'

Elspeth beamed at this and then turned her attention to her niece.

'What are you doing?' she boomed. Tess stopped with her cup halfway to her lips.

'Having a cup of tea?' she offered.

'Why don't you leave Tally here' the dog in question was now asleep under the table ' and go and have a look at Ginn Ghyll Force?'

'What and where is it?' Tess was intrigued as she hadn't heard of it before.

'Our very own waterfall – or spout as we call it round here. You must have passed by the entrance many times. Down by the side of Beaumont's B&B, there's a narrow ginnel and you just follow the stepped stones for a while until you're at the bottom of the ghyll. Then turn left and carry on until you see it. You'll hear it first. It's hidden away and nobody would guess it was there. It's a magical place and you might as well have a look while you have nothing else to do.'

It was a 'blink and you miss it' gateway with steep steps down that seemed to go on forever, formed out of the rock itself. It was possibly treacherous in muddy, wet weather as even in summer, the rock was damp. Occasionally holding on to a rickety fence at the side, she descended to the silent depths, where even the birds seemed too quiet.

How could this be on the moors or what she had imagined the moors to be? Heather, gorse, bracken and vast tracts of undulating land with no trees. Round here at least, it was different. There were surprises everywhere. Green, fertile basins, deep crevasses, tumbling water, high hills and gentle streams. This was the North Yorkshire Moors – a bit of everything.

She reached the bottom – she hoped- and turned left. She could see nothing but twists and turns through sheer rock sides with a fast-running stream coursing through it. The sun was reaching its fingers down and lighting up the ripples on the water. It made her feel incredibly peaceful.

Someone had thoughtfully put a bench set back against the left of the path and she sat there for a while, just enjoying the solitude. Gradually she became aware of a noise further to her left. She stood up and walked, or rather climbed, towards its source. The path had all but disappeared and around the last bend, she saw it. Ginn Ghyll Force. Falling down from the top of the ghyll, it caught jutting rocks on its descent, sending clear sprays of water in all directions. The sun found its way there too, sparkling and dancing on the droplets and… She stopped, then looked closer.

There were lights. A purple colour, lots of different shades of purple, mauve, lilac, lavender. It must have been some sort of natural phenomenon, like a rainbow reflected in the moisture yet…she stepped closer. The lights shifted position as though they were twisting and turning. They were irregular shapes, no two the same. They seemed to move to a beat rather than with the movement of water, The top parts appeared to be translucent? Oh -she needed to get closer. If she could step over these stones to the other side. She took a step forward and her foot slipped from underneath her and she was surrounded by jagged rocks. She shut her eyes.

Suddenly, strong arms were under hers, preventing the fall she was certain was going to happen.

'Are you alright?' came a concerned voice. Luke!

'How on earth did you   ?' gasped Tess.

'Right place, right time' he laughed. 'Were you trying to get a closer look at our fairies?'

165

'What?' she said in a shriller voice than she meant to.

'The purple lights? Our fairies. Not real ones of course. There's a scientific explanation. Some professor gave a talk in the village hall once. Couldn't understand a word he said. You sure you're alright?'

'Sure. I'd feel better on safe, firm ground again though' so they started to walk back. Tess was quiet for a minute then said,

'What do you see?'

'Where?'

'The lights, what do you see?'

'Purple specks of light in the spray. Why, what do you see?' he frowned.

'Same' she lied.

She risked a sidelong glance at him but he seemed satisfied with her answer. He held his hand out to her at a particularly tricky part and she thankfully took it, feeling ridiculously shy. When they reached the more negotiable steps, he didn't let go of her hand and Tess was content to let it stay there.

There was an easy conversation between them with none of his sarcasm and none of her put-downs. It lasted right until they reached the green, where they parted ways. He held her arms and gave her a smile that melted her heart, then leant forward and kissed her forehead tenderly. Tess, trying to smile but feeling awkward, settled for,

'Thank you for saving me on the rocks.'

'I'm just glad I was there. Actually, you should thank Elspeth. It was her who suggested I have a walk to see the Force. I realised I hadn't been for a while so – right place, right time, like I said.'

As they turned in opposite directions, Tess allowed her eyes to narrow and her mouth to settle in a thin line. Her aunt just happening to suggest a walk to them both, ten minutes apart? Coincidence? I don't think so! thought Tess. Elspeth, you are in so much trouble.

Chapter 20

'Hurry up and finish whatever it is you're doing. I want a word with you in my study.'

Elspeth barked out her order and as she usually sounded this way in everyday speech, Tess, had no idea whether she was in trouble or not.

She had tried to impress on Elspeth not to try and make something out of nothing where her and Luke were concerned. Her aunt's insistence that 'It was telling you to look at the ghyll that just reminded me when I saw Lukas' didn't wash with Tess. It sounded too off pat but she could hardly call her aunt out for telling fibs, so she left it.

What she *was* doing, when Elspeth came into Tess's study, was looking for jobs. Again. And still not finding any. She had now become determined to take anything reasonable that came up because she was beginning to feel like a burden, an idler and she couldn't afford to be so picky. Her father had sent her details of an accountancy job quite near to his parish in Norfolk. He had sent an apology saying he knew she didn't want another accountancy job but with it being near home, he thought he'd send it anyway. She looked at it to show willing but she knew in her heart she would rather take a job in Shady O'Rourke's lap dancing club, dressed in a few strategically placed feathers, than go back to accounting. She sighed and made her way to Elspeth's study.

Her reception, oddly, was one of enthusiasm and almost girlishness. Tess wondered again at the power of the ring that her aunt said had restored her energy and confidence. Tess thought it was psychological but, whatever it was, it worked.

'Come and have a look at this' Elspeth said, picking up the top one of a pile of papers on her desk. Tess came round and looked at what seemed to be a plan, roughly drawn in pencil.

'This' her aunt announced proudly, 'is my plan for the barn.'

'The old Folklore Museum barn?' Tess asked stupidly, even though she didn't know of another.

'The *new* Folklore Museum barn' Elspeth replied.

'You're starting up again?' Tess couldn't help smiling at the happy expression on Elspeth's face. She really had got a new lease of life.

'Yes but with a few changes. Look – the main area is to be left open so we can have some living history demonstrations of countryside crafts. I haven't thought about it fully yet. I will also use the space for storytelling sessions for the youngsters and the not so young.

Round the edges will be the artefacts we already have and some more I want to buy but all displayed in a more attractive way to engage their interest more. Perhaps with a couple of interactive displays for the children?

Then the big change. I'd like to put a small café at the back, just basically for drinks and scones, cakes and biscuits. I don't want to take business away from the tea rooms although they do sandwiches, pastries and teacakes as well as cakes, more substantial things. Sally is sometimes overrun with visitors and locals and hasn't got the room for them. I had a word with her yesterday and all she said was 'Can I supply your cakes?' Of course I said yes, they are delicious as you know.

The loos are already in place but need a complete overhaul. I've had a word with the decorators, Danny and Brian, who live in the village and they can start next week. Well, what do you think?'

Tess blinked.

'I think I'm caught up in a whirlwind' she replied honestly 'but I think it's a fantastic idea! I've been sad about the museum being closed and never having had a chance to see it. Especially since I learnt that this area is known to be so important for the tradition of folklore. So many of the legends are based within a seven mile radius with Weaver's Green as its core. It seemed such a waste not to have it up and running.'

'I'm so glad to hear you say that.' gushed Elspeth and very unexpectedly, turned to give her a quick hug. I think my aunt has been replaced by an alien, thought Tess but was pleased nonetheless.

'With your business degree, you can come up with suggestions of how it can all work'

'It focussed more on accounting and finance Elspeth and I think you have plenty great ideas yourself; your creativity seems to have had a fresh surge of energy too. You know, though, that I will be more than pleased to help in any way I can.'

'Excellent.' There was a pause. 'I have to be honest. I *did* suggest that Luke had a walk down the ghyll, knowing you'd be there. It was only a suggestion though, not an order.'

'Even your suggestions are usually spoken in a voice that must be obeyed, Great Aunt.'

Elspeth shot her a mini version of The Look.

'I don't know what you've got against Luke, he's a great favourite of mine.'

'I haven't got anything against him. We get on fairly well now but we're happy as we are, as friends. I think I can speak for us both when I say what is to be, will be. *Without* your matchmaking.'

Elspeth gave an exaggerated sigh and threw her hands up in a gesture of defeat. Her expression changed and she looked back at Tess with a sly glance.

'You saw the lights, did you say? At the waterfall?'

'Yes, I told you.'

'Both of you saw them?'

'Yes, why?'

'No reason' There was a pause. 'What exactly did you see?'

'Like I said, purplish dancing lights in the spray.'

'Did the lights look strange to you at all?'

'Not really. Well, I suppose they…'

'They what?' asked Elspeth, trying to be nonchalant.

'They had – a form. Not just lights They seemed to have different shapes.' As soon as she said it, Tess realised this is what her aunt had been leading her to.

'Of course,' said Elspeth 'I used to call them the original Fairy lights and asked my mother if they would come on our Christmas tree one year. My favourite story of my mother's was Fairies of the Falls. By the way, your father is coming up to see us today.'

This last statement was said in such a throwaway fashion that Tess wasn't sure she'd heard right.

'Dad? But he emailed me yesterday and didn't mention it.'

'Must have been before I phoned him then. He'll be here in time to join us for lunch.

*

The Wykeham Arms was heaving today. A cloudless sky, brilliant sunshine and a determination to enjoy the weather had brought lots of visitors in the direction of Weaver's Green today. Among them was Eustace d'Evreux who was now seated at a table in the corner, where it was cooler than outside. Opposite him sat his Aunt Elspeth while Tess stood at the bar, ordering their food from Des.

She looked back at them fondly. She had never noticed a resemblance between them before but, although Eustace didn't have the 'Wykeham eyes', the bone structure, set of the mouth and the erect posture was the same. As well as the long aristocratic nose. Apparently that was the d'Evreux nose, which she was quite glad she hadn't inherited. Tess wondered if all body parts had to be inherited. 'Oh, you've got the Smither's left knee there' or 'I see you've got the Fanshawe big toe'. Although, in a way, it was awesome to think that these traits or features could have been exactly the same as your ancestors had from a couple of hundred years ago or more.

She came back to the present when Des handed her a wooden block with an order number stuck in it.

'I hope it will be about fifteen minutes but it may be later?' Des indicated the number of people with an apologetic shrug.

'No hurry Des' she smiled and went to sit down.

'So' she began, 'you're witnessing something at the solicitors for Aunt Elspeth?'

'Apparently, things have been thrown into mild disarray with the unexpected developments at Rook Hall. I'm needed to provide another signature-and of course, I'm here to see my lovely daughter who I thought would be back home by now.' Eustace smiled to show this wasn't meant as a slight.

'Don't you go persuading her to return to Norfolk, she's been very helpful here' said Elspeth.

'I'm glad to hear it' replied Eustace, incredulity written on his face.

'Don't look so shocked Dad. I can be useful when I want' Tess laughed.

'It's not that, it's the fact that Elspeth actually accepted help that shocked me.'

'Watch it, young Eustace. Anyway, I think I may have changed. It's possibly down to Tess or to the ring, or both.' Elspeth held her hand out to show off the ring.

'The Balefire Ring!' Eustace obviously had heard of it. 'You got it back then?'

'Thanks to Tess here, who 'saw' where it was.'

You could almost see the inverted commas hovering over Elspeth's head as she put particular emphasis on the word. Tess closed her eyes; she didn't know if she was ready for this.

'Oh don't start all that Aunt Elspeth' said Eustace, looking as pained as his daughter. 'I know there are things in our family that can't be explained but just because they can't now doesn't mean that they won't be, scientifically, one day.'

'Then just think how far ahead of science we are Tess.' She raised her eyebrows and Tess smiled weakly. ' although I'm still trying to persuade your daughter she has inherited the gift.'

'Please don't' said Eustace, wearily.

'This coming from someone who believes in voices from the sky, rivers changing into blood and seas being parted, *Reverend* Eustace?'

'Now then children' Tess jumped in. Although there didn't seem to be any malice intended, she would rather change the subject before it got out of hand. She liked to avoid confrontations where possible. 'Do you want me to drive you to Whitby this afternoon? Give you a rest from driving, Dad?'

'No need unless you want to go in particularly. I can drive your father there in the Porsche.'

Tess looked nervously at her father after Elspeth's statement but he didn't look worried. She concluded that this was because he had never been driven by Elspeth before. She couldn't put him through that.

'It's okay, I could do with getting a few things' said Tess, dishonestly.

'Well actually, I'd rather like a ride in this Porsche' said her father, like a lamb to the slaughter.

'No problem' grinned Elspeth with unnecessary zeal, 'Eat up and we'll be off then.'

Poor dad thought Tess, he doesn't know what he's let himself in for.

Chapter 21

Finding herself at a loose end, Tess got the museum keys from the drawer and walked there. It really was hot outside so it was mercifully cool inside the barn. With her aunt's plans in her mind, she wandered round the place with fresh eyes. The possibilities were so much more evident since the first time she saw it.

If they could get planning permission, a few more windows would be called for to lighten up the place, especially at the café end. The walls, instead of being bare white rough plaster, could have illustrations from each of the local folk tales hung on them.

She imagined all the displays set out differently, leaving a workable space in the middle for Elspeth's storytelling sessions or for demonstrations of the local crafts such as spoon carving, spinning and making rag rugs. Perhaps, on days like today, the double barn doors could be thrown open and the sessions could be held on the grass area out at the front. The children could sit on mats whilst Elspeth sat on a chair in front of them, dressed in a sixteenth-century goodwife's costume.

Depending on how many people Elspeth wanted to seat in the café, there may need to be an extension. Perhaps a conservatory would do? In fact, thought Tess, that would be a good idea. There would be fewer planning problems and they could put trellising and pot plants to brighten the small courtyard which was between the conservatory and the car park. Tess grinned at her own enthusiasm and checked to see that, she too, wasn't wearing a Balefire ring.

As she returned to the entrance, she saw Berry walking along the road. With her were Shah, Steven and someone she hadn't seen before.

'Tess!' yelled Berry, running up to give her a hug. She waved towards the stranger. 'Tess, Brian. Brian, Tess.'

They smiled and nodded at each other.

'We're just going up to measure out the allotments' Berry indicated some sticks and balls of twine they were carrying and Shah held up what looked like Thor's hammer. 'Are you coming with us?'

'Can I just nip back and get Tally? There's some shade under the trees where she can sleep.

It's so hot for her today, she didn't even want to come out for a walk.'

'You are both welcome anytime. If it wasn't for you and Elspeth, we would still have no land.' Berry held up a cool-box in her other hand, licking her lips 'Cold home-made lemonade'

'I'll bring another beaker and a bowl for Tally.'

'Will she like lemonade?' asked Berry seriously.

'I meant for the water I'll be bringing, you nutcase. See you in a minute.'

Tally needed some persuasion to move from the cold kitchen tiles but she needed to go out. When she saw her friends Clover and Daisy in the shade near the hedge, she wanted to join them but Berry had said that although usually docile with humans, donkeys sometimes saw small dogs as a pest and rewarded them with a swift kick in their direction. Tess pulled her onwards towards the others, where she put her bowl down in the shade of the hedge. After going round everyone and having a fuss made of her, she decided that was enough socialising for today and went to lie down next to her bowl.

Four marked-out allotments later, all five of them – six with Tally – stretched out under an elder tree in dappled shade and thankfully drank their lemonade.

'Berry, have you asked Tess yet about, you know?' Shah said, nodding in the general direction of the barn.

'Considering we were only talking about it on the way up…Give me chance!' retorted Berry.

'Ask me? About what?'

'Well, you and Elspeth. We thought maybe you could have a word with her first as most of us – as kind and generous as she has been – are still terrified of getting our heads bitten off.'

'Is it that bad?' Tess was getting worried now.

'No, I, that is we just wondered if we could set up a stall, a bit like my flower stall but bigger, with a striped awning. If we put it at the other side of the gate next to the hedge, we could put any spare produce there with an honesty box with it. What with that and what we get from supplying the village shop, we can pay our peppercorn rents and buy any more seeds that we can't generate ourselves. We should be completely self-sufficient. What do you think?'

'I think it's an excellent idea and I'm sure Elspeth will too. The museum will also be able to provide customers too as they'll see the stall when they visit' enthused Tess.

There was a short silence then Steven said,

'The Folklore Museum? Is it starting up again then?'

Too late, Tess realised that perhaps Elspeth didn't want everyone to know just yet.

'Oh yes, there are plans but only plans just yet. I don't know whether I was supposed to say anything so please don't mention it to anyone will you?'

'We won't breathe a word' whispered Berry and Tess realised this would be a hard task for someone as gregarious as she was.

'Actually' said Brian, 'Miss Wykeham d'Evreux has already phoned me and my cousin Danny about painting the place inside and out.'

Ah, Danny and Brian, the decorators who lived in the village. That rang a bell. She might not get into trouble after all. Tally began nudging Tess and looking distractedly down towards the gate.

'Tally's telling me it's teatime' she laughed. 'I'd better go anyway. Elspeth and her Porsche will be back with my father's feet stuck to the floor still putting the imaginary brakes on.'

They all raised their eyes to heaven or grimaced. Elspeth and her driving exploits were well known around the village. When Tess and Tally reached home. The Porsche was already in the garage and aunt and nephew were in the sitting room with a pot of tea.

Tess fed Tally then brought a fresh pot of tea through along with some fruit scones from Sally's. She told them about the veg and fruit stall idea and, as she guessed, Elspeth totally supported it. She also told them of her thoughts as she had wandered round the museum and of all her own little ideas to add to Elspeth's. She offered to do the illustrations for the walls if her aunt liked the idea but if she found a job, she would still do them and bring them up one weekend. She noticed a look pass between her father and aunt and suddenly remembered their visit to Whitby. She eyed her father for signs of extreme shock but there didn't seem to be any.

'Did everything go well at the solicitor's?' she asked tentatively.

'Fine thank you.'

'Good, good. And – what did you think to the Porsche then?' she asked in what she mistakenly thought was a light-hearted manner.

There was a snort from Elspeth's direction and a knowing smile from her father.

'Aunt Elspeth explained about how much you loved being driven about by her' he said.

Tess looked annoyed at her for exposing her cowardice but Elspeth just carried on chuckling.

183

'To be honest' continued Eustace 'by the time we reached Whitby my knuckles were white from hanging on – but it was exhilarating, It took me back to my younger days.'

'Dad! Just what sort of younger days did you have?'

'I haven't *always* been a vicar you know' he laughed, then cleared his throat. 'I'm driving back home tonight as I have a meeting with the church council at 9 am tomorrow but before I do, I think Elspeth has something she wants to say.'

This sounded ominous, thought Tess. Elspeth was shifting about on her chair in an uncharacteristically nervous fashion.

'I have a proposition for you' she said. 'As you know, I've decided to re-open the Folklore Museum but make it better and more customer friendly – and I'd like you to run it for me. Now before you say anything, it is a fully paid job. While not paying as much as accountancy, it will see you with a decent wage.

I will still be involved and will still do the storytelling sessions but I would also like to travel round the district to schools and groups like I used to, so I need someone here permanently to run the place. Gwen and Olive as well as myself will always be happy to cover for the days you want off. Your ideas you just mentioned are exactly how I would like it. You have the foresight and creativity to make a real success of it. You've been looking for a job, so how about this? In the family firm, so to speak'

There was a pause that seemed to go on forever and Elspeth's smile began to waver. Tess spoke at last.

'Elspeth, if you trust me to make a good job of this enterprise, there is nothing I would like better than to get the museum up and running again – and stay here in this wonderful village. With you.'

Relief spread over Elspeth's face and for the second time that day, she came to give Tess a hug. There was a strong chance if they looked at each other, there may be a damp eye or two.

'Eustace, is that alright with you?' she said, pulling away at last, 'I feel like I'm taking your daughter away from you.'

'Of course it is, she hasn't lived with me for the last eight years.' He laughed, then his face became serious as he looked at Tess. ' Can I just say this? For years, I have regretted talking you out of the art course. I could see afterwards that accountancy wasn't you at all. It stifled your imagination and you weren't happy. I have had enormous feelings of guilt since.

Now, seeing how happy this opportunity and indeed this village, has made you, I am glad to see you in your rightful place, doing what you enjoy.' And he too got up to give Tess a tight hug.

'Dad, I weighed up everything you said, which was practical advice and all you could give, not being able to climb inside my mind, and it was me who made that decision in the end. If I had decided to go to art college, then you wouldn't have been able to stop me. I didn't decide to – so stop feeling guilty. I agreed with you at the time, albeit reluctantly.'

Later that night as she tried unsuccessfully to put everything out of her mind and go to sleep, Tess reflected not only on the offer which had come at exactly the right time before she took a dead-end job out of desperation but also on how well the three family members had got on today. Any rift between her father and his aunt seemed to be healed and they were almost like a normal family now. If normal was the right word for what this family actually was.

Chapter 22

Everyone was standing in the hallway, ready to take a look at the barn in earnest. Brian and Danny were armed to the teeth with colour charts and two plasterers were to meet them there. Tess had a drawing pad with her and Elspeth had her roughly drawn-up plans under her arm and the keys in her hand.

At the moment they were all looking at Elspeth who had just ignored two questions and had her eyes firmly fixed on the floor.

'Elspeth, said Tess quietly.

After a moment she looked up.

'I'm sorry, here are the keys Tess. Can you show everyone inside just to get an idea of the place for now?'

'Aren't you coming?' Tess asked, puzzled.

'No, you go ahead' came the reply.

Tess went outside with the others and then gave the keys to Brian.

'Can you have a general look round and show Geoff and Charlie round too? I'll join you as soon as I can. If I don't, just lock up and put the keys through this letterbox. I think I ought to stay.'

The men nodded their agreement along with the hope that she was alright and disappeared through the gateway while Tess returned to the hallway.

'Elspeth' said Tess gently' I'm not leaving until I know you're okay. What's wrong?'

'There's nothing wrong with me.' She said distractedly, then looked as though suddenly coming to a decision. She used the house phone and Tess could hear it ringing out for at least a minute.

'Come with me' Elspeth said, opening the door 'and ring Lukas on the way. Ask him if he's heard from Gwen this morning.'

Tess looked startled. 'If he hasn't, what shall I say? He'll want to know why I'm asking.'

'Just do it girl, we'll face those problems when we come to them.'

Her aunt's tone was as sharp as it had been when she'd first arrived. Tess rang Luke. Elspeth was heading across the green.

'Answerphone. I've asked him if he's heard from Gwen and to let us know if he has.'

There was no reply from her aunt. A little further on they saw Olive making her way back to her cottage from the direction of Gwen's house.

'Olive!' shouted Elspeth, stopping the woman in her tracks. They hurried up to her.

'Have you been to see Gwen?'

'Yes' answered Olive, tutting, 'but she must have forgotten she invited me round for coffee this morning. She's gone out.'

Elspeth's face went pale.

'Call the ambulance to Gwen's, Olive. Do it now.'

It was a measure of the awe they held Elspeth in that Olive complied with this request immediately, without question.

As they both rushed round to Gwen's, Tess managed to speak.

'What did you 'see', Elspeth?' This no longer seemed a silly thing to say but was just part of her new life.

Her aunt's brows knitted together and she shook her head to dispel the vision.

'She was lying on the floor, blood next to her head.'

Tess ran ahead, alarmed now. For some reason, she felt she had to phone Luke again but instead of an answerphone, she heard Luke's voice.

'Two minutes' he shouted and was gone.

The front door was locked so as Elspeth tried but failed to find something to pick the lock with, Tess went round the back. That door was locked too but she thought she heard something. She couldn't see anything through the window but put her ear against it. There it was again, a very faint cry. She flew round to the front.

'I think she's in the kitchen but I can't get in. Can we break in between us?'

Suddenly, there was the furious roar of an engine, down the road and a car pulled up outside with a screech of tyres. Luke propelled himself down the path, key already in his hand.

'Is she alright Elspeth?' It didn't sound like the confident Luke but like a scared little child.

'I don't know but Tess heard something. Which is good. How did you know?'

'I've been trying to reach her all morning. She was ringing me with an address I needed. That was before work and when I couldn't get hold of her I was worried. I was on a call near here and was going to drop in afterwards and that's when I got Tess's message.'

Luke was now pushing open the kitchen door and there on the floor, under where the sink was, lay Gwen.

'Gran!' he cried out and ran over to her.

'Don't move her Luke.'

'I know, I know.'

Then Gwen opened her eyes.

'I'm sorry to be a nuisance' she gasped.

'Oh thank god' her grandson said, his eyes shining with tears.

'Ring the ambulance Tess. I know Olive will have done so but I want to know how long.'

Tess rang and was told that an ambulance was on its way.

'Twenty minutes, if we're lucky' she relayed to her aunt. 'They want to know what the injuries are?'

Elspeth replied calmly.

'Injury to the front of the head, possible concussion. Patient conscious and talking but weak.'

She put her head next to Gwen to catch her next words. Elspeth squeezed her eyes shut as she heard them and sighed. Luke put his head in his hands before stroking his gran's cheek.

'Laid on the floor overnight. Possible hypothermia, shivering. Possible shock. Wriggle your fingers if you can Gwen... Possible broken arm. Swollen ankle, bad sprain or possible break.' Tess relayed all this to the emergency services and looked on in horror.

At least she was alive even if she was obviously weak. She felt enormously grateful- and safe- because of her aunt's calming presence. Luke, strong capable Luke, was in pieces. Elspeth seemed to know just what to do and even had Gwen smiling.

'Don't worry' she told Luke 'your gran is a tough old bird; she'll be up and about in no time.'

'I'm glad you're here Elspeth' whispered Gwen.

'And so say all of us' gulped Luke.

'Amen to that' added Tess.

*

The ambulance rushed off to Whitby General and Luke got into his car to follow it.

'Thank you Elspeth.' Luke turned to her with heartfelt gratitude. Then he moved across to Tess and enveloped her in a huge hug, more to comfort him, she thought. She gave him a kiss on the cheek and squeezed his hand. They held each other's gaze for a moment, then he dived in his car and shot off.

'Will she be okay?' Tess asked as though she expected Elspeth to know the answer.

'Now I've seen her, I can see that there will be no lasting damage and she will just need plenty of rest to recover. She said she slipped on some water that had splashed from the sink.'

'It's so easily done though, isn't it? I hope it doesn't make her nervous now.'

'I hope it does make her a little nervous, or perhaps more careful' replied Elspeth. 'I love Gwen dearly but she wasn't blessed with a lot of practical common sense. She doesn't think before she does anything, so maybe now she will.'

'Poor Gwen' said Tess, 'don't you start telling her off when you see her.'

Elspeth smiled.

'I won't. I'm not completely heartless you know.'

'You're not heartless at all' replied Tess.

'Come on' said her aunt, locking up with Luke's key. 'Let's go and have a word with the crew at the barn. It will be a while before Gwen's arm is set and she has had all the necessary examinations. We'll take over from Luke later on but for now, let's see if we can set our minds to our project for a while.'

Chapter 23

As it turned out, neither of them could keep their minds on the museum refurbishment. The plasterers said they would get on with replastering the walls. Danny and Brian just left Elspeth with all their colour charts, hoped Gwen would be alright, and would be back in a couple of days.

'Shall we go to the hospital now?' asked Tess. They couldn't get Luke on his phone but it would probably be turned off inside the hospital.

'You go in your car' said Elspeth decisively. 'Luke will probably be glad of a little moral support. I'm going back to Gwen's to get her some nighties, underwear and toiletries. I expect they will keep her in a little while.'

Tess didn't complain this time at being thrust into Luke's company as she herself felt like he needed moral support. She bought a ham sandwich and a chicken pasty for him from Sally's tea shop in case he hadn't eaten and got herself a cheese and salad roll.

She pulled into the hospital car park and went up to the reception desk.

'Gwen Mills?' she said and received instructions that she would never remember in a month of Sundays. If she followed the coloured line on the floor though, she should be okay.

Eventually, after asking any passers-by who were wearing any sort of uniform, including, memorably, a fireman – she saw Luke sitting in a corridor, his elbows on his knees while he stared at the floor. She went up to him, a worried expression on her face.

'Luke, is everything alright?'

He looked up and gave her a brief smile.

'She's still in surgery. It was a bad break. Luckily it was her left arm but she's still going to be out of action for a while.'

'What about her head?' asked Tess.

'Superficial. It looked worse than it was but it still looks a mess. Her ankle is just badly bruised and sprained but not broken, thank goodness.'

'I can't believe' said Tess, 'that your broken limb has only just healed and now your gran has got one.'

'I know, we seem to be pretty accident-prone don't we?' he said with a grimace. 'Gran looked after me when I had my accident and now I'm going to move in and look after her.'

Tess smiled to herself, thinking of the first and evidently very wrong impression she had of him. He was sensitive and kind but he liked to hide it under a bluff and sarcastic exterior. At least, until he got to know you.

'Do you mean permanently?' she asked.

'For the foreseeable future at least' he confirmed.

'You do realise your love life will go out of the window when you can't take the ladies back to your flat after a night out being wined and dined on the town?' she shook her head solemnly. At the same time, she was asking herself if this was really a joke or whether she was fishing for information.

'There might just be some ladies in the village who would be interested in being wined and dined at the Wykeham Arms with a Chicken Balti and a cuddle on the bench on the green.' He was smiling now, whether or not he really understood her meaning more than she did herself. The tension eased slightly. The next second he sat bolt upright as a nurse came towards him.

'Mr. Mills? Your grandmother is awake now and sitting up in bed if you'd like to see her?'

'Is she alright?'

'She's as good as can be expected, just a little tired, that's all.'

Luke grinned at Tess and they followed the nurse as she showed them along another corridor and into a ward. In one of the first side wards, Gwen sat, propped up on pillows.

'Luke dear, could you pop out and buy me another nightie? They've got me in one of these hospital things and they barely cover your modesty. It will have to button up the front though and be sleeveless because of my arm.'

Tess took one look at Luke's appalled expression at the thought of going shopping for women's nightwear, and put him out of his misery.

'It's okay Gwen, Elspeth's coming over with some nighties and other stuff you may need. She'll know to make sure at least one is sleeveless.'

She heard Luke exhale with relief next to her.

'Well, nothing seems to put you off your stride does it gran?' He smiled at her completely unworried face.

'Can't do anything about it so I may as well be happy as miserable. Although it might be a bit difficult coping at first when I get home.' She didn't look at Luke when she said this but left a pregnant pause, hoping it would be filled with what she wanted to hear. Luke and Tess looked at each other and Luke winked.

'I'm coming to stay at yours again to look after you. You can't seem to get rid of me, can you?'

'That would be very nice love, if you're sure you can manage it. I don't want to get in the way of your life, you know.'

'Oh, in that case, I'll just ask Tess here to look in now and again instead. Would that be better?'

Gwen looked at him and grinned.

'It's a good job I know you better than that Luke Mills but I really do appreciate it.'

'Although' Luke frowned 'I *am* back at work now, so I might really have to ask people to look in on you when I'm not there. A home help comes in for the first week I think, if you want them?'

'I'm grateful for any help I receive.' Gwen patted his hand.

'And I'm sure there will be no shortage of people in the village willing to give that help, including me - and Elspeth of course' said Tess.

'You're a good girl, isn't she Luke?'

'Yes gran' he replied, raising his eyes.

Oh god, thought Tess, he's had the same treatment from Gwen as I've had from Elspeth. It was more likely to push them apart than together.

They all chatted for a while until Gwen finally nodded off. They held a whispered conversation over her as Luke had to call the station. Asking for a few days off when his gran went home, after being off for weeks before, wasn't a conversation he was looking forward to. He went outside with his mobile and just when Tess had given up on him, he came back.

'The boss says it's fine and these things happen but he'll have to terminate my employment afterwards.'

Tess's face registered horror and disbelief. Just disbelief would have done as a wide grin spread across his face.

'Only joking'

'You're back to normal, I see' her tone implied that it wasn't entirely a good thing.

'How is she?' came Elspeth's voice from the doorway.

'Asking for a decent nightie' laughed Luke.

They filled her in on events and then Luke said he'd have to get back to the station to sort things out.

'You get off too Tess. I'll stay here with her now and Tally will want her dinner soon. I'll see you later.'

Tess and Luke walked to the car park together then he turned towards her, planting a gentle kiss just that bit too close to her lips.

'Thank you for being there Tess' and he rushed off to his car leaving Tess smiling inanely to herself.

Chapter 24

Gwen wasn't long before she was back home with a small army of helpers all taking turns to go and check on her. Luke was staying there and brought her shopping home but Olive, Des, Shep and Shep's sister Della made sure they both had a home-cooked meal on an evening. Luke thought his gran was enjoying the attention a little too much and told her not to get used to it as she would soon be back looking after him instead. She hit him with her good arm and he grinned. They were enjoying each other's company again but agreed that they had better not break a limb every time to do so.

Elspeth had put a small poster on the village hall noticeboard regarding a general meeting, then sent her niece round all the houses in the village with a slip of paper to post through their letterboxes. Along with the restoration of the museum, her aunt had a new project on the go. She couldn't seem to sit still. Tess thought about hiding the ring for a while so she slowed down for a while but she was so energetic and happy that she liked this new-style great aunt.

The evening of the meeting, when it arrived, was a balmy, sleepy, golden kind of evening where the heat was soporific rather than intense and the light was mellow. It was lucky it was, thought Tess, as the meeting was being held on the green with no alternative venue. Almost as if her aunt had known it would be good weather. She threw a sharp glance at her aunt who gave her a puzzled smile back. No, don't be silly Tess, she thought.

Everyone was walking towards the bench at the edge of the green, carrying a folding chair or a blanket. They were setting them down as Tess and her aunt arrived. Gwen sat on the bench with Luke on the grass by her side. Elspeth put her chair up at the other side of the bench and this seemed to be the focal point that everyone turned towards.

'Can you all see me – or at least hear me?' said Elspeth in her schoolmistress's voice.

'They can hear you over in Whitby' said Luke as everyone laughed.

'Did somebody speak?' asked Elspeth, studiously ignoring him.

Everyone was smiling, obviously used to the banter. After a couple of minutes, as Elspeth waited for a few last-minute stragglers, she began.

Firstly, can I introduce you to what will be our new neighbours at Rook Hall, Kevin and Sharon Brown'

Everyone shouted their greetings to the new couple and their two children. Tess's eyes widened as she saw them stand up. She hadn't recognised them as they weren't in their Goth persona. Their hair was black but apart from that, they looked remarkably ordinary in jeans and tee shirts. Kevin came and stood by Elspeth, who nodded.

'Hi everyone. These are our children, Lucien and Branwen who will go to the local primary school. We are all looking forward to moving here as soon as we can. I just want to give you a heads-up that we will be having paying guests as we intend Rook Hall to be a Gothic Experience guesthouse. We guarantee that it won't interfere with your village at all and we don't bite – even if some of us have specially-made Dracula fangs for the Goth festivals' he smiled 'We just want to join in with village life and run Rook Hall as a hobby, as I'm a builder by trade. Elspeth has already booked me for alterations to the museum.'

There was a ripple of laughter at this as it was well known that Elspeth was a hard woman to say no to.

'We already knew about the plans for Rook Hall and nobody objects.' Shah shouted out. 'You'll find the village grapevine is quicker than any announcements!'

They all laughed as they acknowledged this. Kevin continued.

'So, thanks to you all for your welcome and to Elspeth for telling us about our dream house. I promise we are a normal family - well almost – and that there will be no black magic going on there!' he laughed and the others joined him. One wag, possibly Danny, thought Tess, shouted out,

'We leave the black magic up to Miss Wykeham d'Evreux here. When I was a kid she used to turn me into a quivering jelly just by looking at me.'

Elspeth, luckily, laughed louder than anyone else, except perhaps for Tess – who had been on the receiving end of those 'looks' on more than one occasion. Kevin went to sit down with his family while Elspeth took over again.

'Now, you will all have seen the notice by now outside the village hall. Most of you here will remember the Halloween festivities we were famous for. The whole village used to celebrate together and welcome anybody who wanted to join us. Kevin and Sharon were two of those people who remembered it fondly and came here regularly.

You will also know that Tess and I have plans to completely overhaul the old Folklore Museum but with the best will in the world, we will not be open before Halloween. We can open for our first viewers on that day and of course, revive the All Hallow festival.

This got me thinking of the old traditions of Weaver's Green and this area. Many of you older ones might remember the other folk festivals we used to have. The Ostara festival in Spring and the Apple Day folk festival at the end of summer. We used to have it on the last weekend before the children returned to school for the autumn term, so, end of August – beginning of September. It was when we could harvest much of the fruit, depending on the variety. Apples, pears, damsons, greengages, raspberries and redcurrants – all anyone could spare from their own trees and bushes were brought to be sold, given and swapped or made into pies and tarts.' There was a murmur of assent and people nodded to each other in recognition of shared memories.

'This is how apple-bobbing originated, originally through Apple Days and not Halloween and there are many more games and activities I remember from when my mother used to run them. So…how about we revive this tradition and bring our community and neighbouring ones together in celebration?

There would be traditional folk music and as dusk arrives, storytelling round the camp fire. What do you think everyone? Elspeth waited a few seconds before Sally spoke up.

'I do a mean spiced toffee and apple cake.' She said as everyone went 'Ooh' and licked their lips.

'Perfect' said Elspeth.

'I know a folk band who would be happy to come here, they've played at the pub before.' said Des and Elspeth asked if he would get in touch with them. 'and that place in the next valley makes its own cider, I could ask them about taking part too.' added Des.

'How about swapping apple tree cuttings, there are different varieties people might want to try. It would maintain the old English varieties too.'

'Good idea George – I'll leave that to you to organise'

'I think it would look magical on the green with some fairy lights hanging in the trees? ' said Tess.

'It would – and I'll let you organise that too. Anyone else who wants to be a helper, just get in touch with us. The more the merrier.

As it will be held here on the village green as usual, we are dependent on the weather but I'm sure it will be fine. It will be a chance for our community and our neighbours to get together. We seem, as a country, to have lost the capacity for unbridled enjoyment and fun for its own sake. It could be a chance to welcome others here again to our village. We have always welcomed strangers, all the way back to taking in the Weaver himself and providing him with a home – and may we always do so. I am proud of this village and of all of you and I think we deserve a huge celebration. What do you say?'

There was a roar of approval and a round of applause for this impassioned speech.

'And so say all of us' George called out. 'I used to love Apple Day!'

Everyone started coming up to Elspeth with ideas and offers of help. Tess had already pledged her help in whatever way she could but was now thinking about the story of the Weaver that Elspeth had mentioned. She must read her aunt's book so she could get some ideas for the illustrations for the museum walls. She needed some large canvases and some acrylic paint and paintbrushes. She was really looking forward to this. She hadn't painted since she left school and now found that her passion for it hadn't abated.

She felt, rather than saw, someone at her shoulder and turned round to see Luke. His slow, easy smile made her stomach flip, to her annoyance.

'Are you helping at this Apple Day then?' he asked.

'Of course and Elspeth didn't even have to order me to. I'm looking forward to it.'

'Hmm,' Luke lifted an eyebrow.

'What?'

'Well I asked gran and she said the tradition was that all the helpers and stallholders had to dress up. She thinks Elspeth may still have the costumes somewhere. It was part of the fun.'

Did he think she was so buttoned-up?

'That's alright, I don't mind dressing up' she retorted.

'As an apple?' he said.

There was a pause.

'You're kidding me' she laughed expectantly, waiting for him to say he was joking.

His face was apologetic.

'Apparently, it's tradition. The costumes are padded out so you're slightly rounded and there's a hat with a stalk on it. Kiddies and adults regardless have to do it. Part of the fun – or so they say.' He winced then shrugged and walked away.

Tess stood there horrified. Tradition or not, there was no way she was dressing up as an apple, especially with a stalk on her head. As soon as she got Elspeth alone, she was going to ask her to veto this particular part of the festival. She looked up and saw Elspeth walking in her direction.

'I'm not going to be an apple!' she shouted towards her.

'Good' said Elspeth, not missing a beat, 'I'm glad we've got that sorted. Now you can tell me why you thought you should be an apple in the first place.'

Tess slowly turned to the bench to see Luke and Gwen laughing like drains and wiping their eyes.

Tess thought of encasing Luke's head in an apple pie. She then thought that she might think this was all funny tomorrow. Probably.

Meanwhile, she walked over to Berry for a bit of relatively normal conversation.

Chapter 25

Tess managed to get one of the canvasses in the car but the other five were being delivered. She just wanted to get on painting this one which is why she was struggling down the slippery, cobbled streets of Whitby on the only rainy day in nine days with a large square canvas, wrapped in black plastic. She had already narrowly avoided taking out someone's eye as she manoeuvred it round a corner and then she had slapped a small man on the back of his head as she turned to see if the road was clear. Fortunately, he was very polite and even raised his hat at her as she apologised profusely, then had guided her across the road, holding on to her arm. She felt like a cross between a near-sighted old lady and a small child on a school outing.

Having safely slid the precious cargo along the back seats and put her rucksack filled with acrylic paints and paintbrushes in the boot, she set off to find her aunt who had gone to the library. She was also putting a poster for the Apple Day folk festival on their noticeboard and making enquiries about giving a talk on the traditions of Apple Day on the North Yorkshire moors to drum up some interest for the actual day.

Tess saw her aunt through the glass door, bending over a table full of leaflets, with a bag full of books on the floor by her side. As Tess opened the door, Elspeth turned to give her a little wave. At this moment, a figure waved back from behind another glass door to the right. The woman shot out through the door, grabbed Elspeth's arm and said urgently,

'Are you the speaker?' the woman squealed.

'Well, I suppose I am… I wanted a word with someone…' said Elspeth, thrown from her usual self-possession by the woman's strange behaviour.

'Oh thank goodness, I thought we'd have to give you up for lost. No explanations now, though I do think you could have let us know, as you're over twenty minutes late starting your talk. You'll have to cut it short I'm afraid, they were just about to leave. Couldn't you find us? Was it the traffic…?'

The voice emanating from an extremely thin woman with Judi Dench hair, just kept wittering on as she dragged Elspeth over to what a sign announced as Community Room. Elspeth whispered over her shoulder to Tess,

'Have I passed into an alternative world?'

The woman pushed her through in a panic and Tess saw a large poster on the open glass door advertising the talk supposed to be taking place now. It was 'How to get Creative with your Cat'. Tess groaned and thrust a flyer from the inside table into Elspeth's hands. Elspeth looked at her and Tess shook her head, meaning, 'Get out of this now.'

As the woman was announcing her, apologetically, Elspeth looked down at the title on the flyer, which also showed one cat wearing a knitted waistcoat and another having a knitted mouse dangled in front of it. She looked back at Tess with an expression of pure horror as she found herself standing in front of a motley crew of about fifteen women.

Audience and victim stared at each other for a moment until Elspeth took one last look at the flyer and caught Tess's eye. A wicked grin appeared on her face. Oh god, thought Tess, she's actually going to enjoy this and she slunk to the back of the room, trying to make herself disappear into the blue plastic chair.

'Ladies, hello' said Aunt Elspeth for all the world like she had been the speaker they expected. She got a very muted response to the greeting and more than a few grumbles.

'You're here to find out how to get creative with your cat. You apparently want to make clothes for your cat and little knitted toys to keep it happy?'

A few people sat up with puzzled looks on their faces, surprised at her tone.

'My question is...Why? Why on earth would you want to dress a creature who has never lost all its wild tendencies in cute little outfits?'

There was a murmur going round the room which didn't seem entirely friendly. Tess risked a glance at their hostess who had pulled them in. Her eyes and her mouth were wide open.

'No, leave the poor cat alone to be a cat without clothes. If the cat could talk it would tell you exactly what you could do with the clothes you have spent a few hours slaving over. Imagine having to wash the blood of the mice and rats it catches, out of its little waistcoat every day.

Don't dangle a knitted mouse in front of it where it will just flick a paw at it because that's what is expected. Get a real live one from your garden. At least it will get a bit of sport while it chases it round your kitchen.'

There were shocked gasps of outrage from the front row – obviously the most avid fans of cat clothes. Tess had a desperate urge to laugh, especially as the hostess's mouth could now admit a small truck. Luckily, she saw two women in front of her turn to each other and grin in delight.

'If you really want to get creative with your cat, buy a large canvas and put it on the floor. Stand the cat in trays of different coloured paints and let it loose across the canvas. Your cat will have a rare old time and you'll be able to sell it to a London gallery for thousands of pounds as the 'latest thing to hit the art scene'.

Now the two in front had really started laughing and others were joining them. Either they loved the irreverence, thought they had a madwoman amongst them, or thought it was a comedy event in the first place.

'Or' continued Elspeth relentlessly, 'to encourage yet more creativity, let your cat loose on your laptop. Let it run backwards and forwards over your keyboard and then try to make some sense out of it every night. Your cat may be a literary genius. It could take thirty years using this method but at the end of it, you'll have a best seller and a work of literary excellence to rival James Joyce 'Ulysses'. In fact, it is claimed he used his cat Tiddles to produce that particular work in exactly this way.'

That was it for Tess, she just burst out laughing, with most of the W.I. joining her, aware now that this was a major mickey-take and this was most definitely not the original event. The clique on the front row, who were obviously expecting some cat-clothes patterns, looked grim and suitably offended.

'Miss Pilmoor!' squeaked the hostess, inching towards Elspeth. 'I do think your flippancy...'

'Who did you say?' asked Elspeth innocently.

'Miss – Miss Pilmoor?' gulped the woman.

'Oh dear, you seem to have dragged the wrong person in to do the talk.'

'But – you said you were the speaker.'

'I am A speaker. In fact, I am scheduled to give a talk on 'The League of Satan and the Naked Covens; How to get discount off your membership'.

More raucous laughter which Tess joined in with, while the front five members walked out in disgust, with the hostess trying to pacify them all the way. Elspeth started to walk towards the door but got a round of applause from what was left of the audience, which she accepted with a curtsey.

'Least boring talk I've ever been to' said one to her neighbour.

Elspeth and Tess reached the freedom of the other side of the main door, grinning at each other like lunatics. The hostess had obviously got up her nose in the first place and the contents of the poster made it even worse. There was no mercy from Elspeth in this mood.

The two women who had been sitting in front of Tess caught them up.

'Miss Wykeham d'Evreux! I knew I recognised you from somewhere I used to come to your Halloween nights at Weaver's Green, right until they finished.'

'And my children used to love listening to your storytelling sessions at St. Hilda's school' said the other. 'I used to be a teaching assistant and I was as enthralled as they were.'

'You haven't lost your storytelling touch have you?' laughed the first woman.

'No I haven't, I'm glad to say, nor my sense of the ridiculous. I really enjoyed that although I think I will be banned from here in future.'

'Were you thinking of joining the W.I. here then Elspeth?' asked Tess, wryly.

'If the usual subjects for talks is knitting clothes for cats, then I'd rather boil my head. Although I hope they're going to let me give a talk on the folk festival.

'Are you starting your Halloween festivals again then? They were great fun. We all looked forward to them.'

'We will be. My niece Tess and I are reopening the much improved Folklore Museum again and the opening will be on Halloween this year.'

The women greeted this with glee.

'Before that though, we are having an Apple Day Folk Festival, reviving an old tradition of the village. There will be music, apples, crafts, food, apples, cider, apples and storytelling on the green'

'With apples?' grinned Tess.

'With apples' agreed Elspeth. 'The details are on a poster in the library. Everyone is welcome so tell all your friends about it. And the rest of the W.I. when they've recovered.'

The two women loved this idea. One of them saying her gran had told her all about the Apple Day that she used to celebrate when she was younger. They went off, chatting excitedly.

'Well' said Tess as they headed for the car park, 'Storyteller, visionary, saleswoman or wind-up merchant? Stand up the real Aunt Elspeth.'

'Don't they all boil down to the same thing?' smiled Elspeth 'Did you get the art stuff for the story panels at the museum?'

'Yes, most of it is being sent on but I'm going to illustrate the first story on the one I'm taking home with me.'

'The Weaver's Tale?'

'Yes, although the next one will be the Black Dog legend, the Gytrash of Godesmere. I'm using Tally as a model. I'll have to use my imagination as she's such a cute little dog so I'll paint her bigger and more horrible in looks, with fangs dripping blood, terrible claws and bright red eyes. I'll think of it as the canine part of Tally with the dread disposition of its owner.' Tess put her head down as she opened the car door.

'Seems like we've got the makings of another storyteller in the family' smiled Elspeth, giving her the heavy bag of books to put in the boot as a punishment.

Chapter 26

'I look stupidly happy don't I?' asked Berry.

'Not stupidly at all. Divinely happy perhaps? I'm so pleased for you Berry. I know you tried to keep it quiet but it was blindingly obvious to everyone. Didn't you realise?' laughed Tess.

'Honestly? No! You just think you've managed to keep a lid on it until everyone informs you afterwards that it was an open secret.'

'So you're moving into the pub with Des then?' asked Tess. 'Are you going to help him run it?'

'I'll be helping out but he's quite happy for me to continue selling my flowers on the stall on the green and at market. He doesn't want to do Shelley out of any hours either as she's worked there for years. I'm very happy about it as I much prefer being in the open air to being inside.'

'Are you getting married?'

'He hasn't asked and I'm not sure what my answer would be if he did. I love him very much and would love children with him but I'm still not sure we need to be married. We'll go with the flow. If we do though, you can be bridesmaid.' Berry smiled.

'Mmm – not a peach blancmange-style dress I hope?'

'Jeans and a pink 'I'm a bridesmaid' tee-shirt?'

'Only one point ahead of the blancmange' scowled Tess.

Berry was quiet for a whole minute, which got Tess worried. Eventually she spoke.

'I was wondering... I will be wanting to rent my cottage out when I move in with Des. It does actually belong to the pub so Des has been *my* landlord as well as *the* landlord. It was fun when he came to collect the rent.' Berry wiggled her eyebrows. 'I remember you saying you loved it so I thought I'd give you the first chance?'

Tess was taken aback; it was so unexpected.

'I mean, I know you get on better with the Drago...with Elspeth now but I thought, if you were going to be staying here that you might like your own space?'

Tess blew out her cheeks.

'Would you believe I truly don't know? I do love your cottage and would have jumped at the offer normally but, living at Wykeham Grange, it is like living separately from Elspeth. We share the kitchen and conservatory but we leave each other alone apart from meals. So I'm torn. Can I have a little time to think about it?'

Berry had been watching her with a disbelieving expression on her face which implied that Tess must be crazy to want to share a house with her mad aunt. Although everyone would have to agree that Elspeth had changed for the better recently.

'It will be a couple of weeks until I can sort out what I'm taking and what I'm getting rid of. The only thing I'm bothered about are the flowers I grow in the garden.'

'Well, if I moved in, you could continue to grow them there as far as I'm concerned' said Tess.

'Aw, thank you. I hope you *do* want it then. The only other thing is to take one of the new allotments up at the top of the field as well. Des says he'll pay for it. I'm looking forward to making hanging baskets for the pub too.'

'Look, I'll have a word with Elspeth without actually saying I'm thinking about moving. I'll sound her out.'

'I suppose it makes sense though, you staying there. I mean, the Grange will be yours eventually I expect, with her not having children?'

Tess sat up as the words struck home.

'I honestly hadn't even thought about that.' Then she sat back and smiled. 'Mind you, after all the palaver about Curwen's inheritance, I wouldn't take anything for granted. Knowing Elspeth, she'll probably leave it to the Institute for Psychic Research. It's hers to do with as she wishes.'

Berry was lost in thought.

'The only other person I'd like to rent my little cottage to is Luke' she said. 'Gwen's house is much smaller than the Grange and they will have no privacy as such. He would only be two hundred yards away round the corner from her if he had this.'

'Berry, that is a brilliant idea and practical too. I know he hates his flat in Whitby. Please ask him first as I think his need is greater than mine. Unless Elspeth decides to kick me out. Don't tell him you offered it to me first or he'll do his 'gentleman' bit. 'Oh no, let Tess have it if you've asked her first.''

You think he cares about your feelings then?' Berry smirked.

'What? No! You know what I mean' said a flustered Tess.

'A gentleman? You think he'll be that polite then?'

'Probably not' answered Tess, just wanting the moment to pass, forgetting this was Berry she was talking to.

'So –' began Berry, 'do you think Luke does like you then?' There was an impish expression on her face.

'No I do not! I never said that. We're just, well not even friends really. I thought he was insufferably rude when I first met him. We just...get on, slightly, because our elders are friends. I've never thought about him – we've never thought about each other like that. At all. I just...'

'Whoa, rein in the runaway horse. You're protesting too much' laughed Berry. 'Remember, you're talking to another one who is obviously rubbish at keeping her feelings secret.'

'But I really don't...' said Tess then pulled on the reins. 'Nothing has been said on either side. Honestly.'

'I believe you because you're both a bit buttoned up emotion-wise if you don't mind me saying, so I shouldn't be surprised. I think though that your inherited second-sight is letting you down in this case. Perhaps you're too close and can't see the wood for the trees?'

'Are you after my aunt's job as wise-woman of Weaver's Green, Berry?'

They both laughed and Tess tried hard not to think of the previous conversation.

'Do you think there really is something in this sort of spooky power that Miss Wykeham d'Evreux has?' asked Berry seriously. 'I mean, everyone in the village seems to take it as read. She has apparently saved people's lives with her, well, I've heard she calls it intuition but it's remarkably strong intuition if so.'

Tess thought for a moment.

'My father is a vicar. I was brought up in the church's ways and although I all but abandoned it as I grew older, the biases are still there. Or were, when I first came here. I scoffed at the stories and like my father – lovely as he is – I thought there was something dark and sinister in visions, seers, second-sight... I thought it was pagan black magic.'

'Pagan doesn't mean black magic you know' remarked Berry. 'It means nature and communing with that nature. It means getting back to the earth, the land, the elements.'

I realise that now. I think it is my father who is misguided in not opening his mind to other possibilities. I know now that Elspeth isn't a witch with a broomstick and a familiar.'

Berry laughed and Tess joined in.

'That's what I was convinced she was when I was younger, mostly because she scared the hell out of me.'

'She still *does* scare the hell out of me' said Berry.

'There's definitely something,' Tess continued, 'I don't know, I can't explain it. I'd like to say she was just eccentric – which she most definitely is – but it goes beyond that. You say she has saved people's lives. I'm convinced she saved Gwen's life because I could see the thought processes she went through beforehand. I knew she was 'seeing' something. There's no doubt she saw what had happened to Gwen.'

'And you, how do you feel about inheriting this gift?'

'Oh, I'm not sure you can say that. A couple of lucky guesses…'

'I don't know if you're in denial more about your gift or about Luke.' Berry stared intently at her; one eyebrow raised.

Tess sighed.

'What are you doing for Apple Day then?' she asked her friend, desperately trying to change the subject again and hoping she'd take pity on her.

'Madame Bernadette's fortune-teller's booth'

'Really?' said Tess.

'No, not really' grinned Berry. 'I'm helping Des with the cider stall. Dressed as an apple.' She looked sideways at Tess and laughed.

'You've been talking to Luke, haven't you?' sighed Tess.

Chapter 27

'I need your help' Luke announced.

They were outside the Wykeham Arms where he had arranged to meet Tess in a text an hour before. It was early evening and the sun was still shining though with less intensity than earlier. It was one of those evenings where everyone felt at peace with the world. A laid-back, forget-your-troubles kind of evening. Tess hoped that wasn't going to change.

'Of course, if I can. Is it Gwen?'

'No. Well, only peripherally anyway. She's fine. Constitution of an ox, like your aunt said. No it's just...' he paused, uncharacteristically unsure of himself. 'Berry has offered to let me rent her cottage. Well her and Des's cottage I suppose – and I'm not sure.'

'What are you not sure about?' asked Tess, trying not to feel a little disappointed.

'About how gran would feel, mostly.'

'Just ask her. No good wondering when you can get the answer from the horse's mouth. She'll probably miss you at first. I suppose she felt safe with you there but you wouldn't be far away.'

'But that's just it. I know gran and I joke about looking after each other with our broken limbs and we *do* get on really well. It's just that really, we are both private and independent people and I'm not sure she'd want me round the corner from her. She'd think I was keeping an eye on her because she's decrepit and we know she's anything but. Also, I would like to come back and live in the village but do I really want to take a backward step?'

This was quite revealing. Tess thought Gwen wouldn't want Luke to move out but she was probably packing his stuff right now.

'From Gwen's point of view, I think Berry's cottage would be an ideal compromise and a definite improvement on you both getting under each other's feet. She's not getting any younger and although independent, I'm sure having her much loved grandson living in the village would be a bonus.

As for you not taking a backward step, how can it be backward when it is something you quite obviously want to do? Backward only as coming back – not a backward step. You don't worry about what others may say, do you? Do what makes *you* happy.'

Luke took her hand in his across the table and smiled warmly.

'Thank you Tess. You've just said exactly what I hoped you'd say and it has confirmed my feelings about moving here'

Tess felt inordinately pleased with herself.

'The only other obstacle,' frowned Luke 'was that Berry said she'd asked you first and you weren't sure?'

So much for Berry not telling him, thought Tess.

'I need to know I'm not taking your cottage for you to use as a refuge from Elspeth the Great? If so, we could always move in together?'

Even though he had said this with an exaggerated wink, Tess blushed from her hair roots to her breastbone.

'I'm absolutely sure I don't want it. I would, as it's lovely but I do love my rooms at the Grange and it's rather nice getting to know Elspeth too. I'm very content where I am.'

'If that's okay then?'

'I mentioned the cottage was for rent and why. Elspeth latched on straight away, asking if I wanted to take it. I said truthfully that I was happy to stay there if she'd have me. She looked mutedly pleased – you'll know the expression- and said that I was welcome to stay as long as I wanted to. Her home was my home. So – no worries on that score.'

'Great, I'll get in touch with Berry tomorrow. Or – and I keep forgetting this – I can tell Des, who can let Berry know' laughed Luke.

'Did you know about them being a couple before then?' she asked.

'It was hard not to with them both gazing into each other's eyes at every conceivable moment. At least, when they thought no one was looking. Of course, we *were* looking and having a good gossip about it too. Ah, the joys of living in a village community, you can't keep anything a secret around here.'

'By the way Luke, how is your allotment coming along?'

'All dug over and just waiting for me to plant my leeks, spring cabbage and turnips.'

'Man of the Land! I wouldn't have had you down as an allotment owner.'

'Perfect foil for my job. Police work takes itself very seriously, as it should. There are some fraught days doing what we are supposed to do, chasing and catching criminals as well as solving robberies and fraud cases. Yet a lot of the time – too much of the time – is taken up with drug-related crimes. Ranging from trying to catch the dealers who have a detrimental effect on the younger community, to drug-related driving incidents, with robberies and muggings just so they can get their drug money.

It's all so dispiriting, it makes you despair of the world today. Knowing that I can come back to this village and get my hands in the soil, plant seeds and watch them grow and just listen to the birds sing as I do it... Not only will I enjoy having an allotment, I think I need it.'

This was the longest speech Tess had heard from Luke and in the space of it, she found that she understood him far better than before.

'Do you ever think of giving the police up?'

'Sometimes but then I'd be like a rat deserting a sinking ship, wouldn't I? I'm one of those disillusioned people who still think they can make a difference.'

Luke smiled ruefully then, changing the mood, asked if she'd like to see his allotment, adding that it made a change from 'Would you like to see my etchings?'. On their way up he asked her if she really was happy to stay here and run the Folklore Museum. Was it creative enough for her?

'Oh yes, I'm sure it is. Creative doesn't always mean the Arts. It also means creating something that people will enjoy and thinking of different ways to achieve that. Elspeth and I have been planning all sorts of events such as school visits, open days and craft days. It's really exciting.'

'I can see that' said Luke, smiling at Tess's enthusiasm.

At the 'top field' as they had all taken to calling it, Luke showed her the allotments, all dug out and in various stages of development. They'd had a few enquiries about the top allotments too, including another one for Berry's flowers, so they would probably be in use too, in the near future.

'We're not having individual huts; it would cost twice as much as one larger communal one. So we're having it in that top corner. It will have plenty of room to store tools and equipment at either end, each with separate entrances, then the middle part with glazed double doors would be a place to gather if it's pouring down so we can boil a kettle on the large primus stove we're clubbing together for, have a cup of tea and put the world to rights.'

'Wouldn't you just go home if it's pouring with rain or not come in the first place?'

'We have Yorkshire grit! Having a cup of tea in your hut while *temporarily* sheltering from the rain is part of the attraction. We've even got a sign in mind to hang up – 'You don't have to be mad to dig in the rain, you just have to be an allotment owner.'

Chapter 28

A contented smile spread across Tess's face. Tally put her head to one side in puzzlement as she wondered, not for the first time, what made humans tick. The human in question was now surveying the canvas in front of her. She had set up her easel in a corner of the large conservatory at Wykeham Grange, where the light was good and unencumbered by overhead vines.

She had just completed her sixth canvas – The Fairies of the Fall. She had been in two minds about how to portray the purple lights, as animated forms as she had seen them or as fairies as most people saw them from childhood. As the story she was illustrating was about fairies, she decided on the latter with a little bit of compromise.

She couldn't help thinking of Luke and his strong arms gripping her as he'd saved her from slipping on the rocks. They were nothing more than friends with no indication from either of them about anything more, yet she was definitely warming to the man. He was one of those people who were much better for knowing and a lesson in not judging people on first appearances.

Creating these artworks had been very therapeutic for her and accounts and finance had started to disappear into a life forgotten. Although those skills would still come in handy when running the museum. She knew that now she had started painting again, that she would continue to do so. Whether as a hobby or something more, she didn't know yet but it didn't matter at the moment. They had the Folklore Museum to finish for Halloween, the actual Halloween celebration to plan – and before that was the Apple Day Folk Festival.

She couldn't believe the contrast with her earlier life. Bored out of her skull with her day job and work acquaintances who she couldn't call friends. They weren't close enough to talk to if she felt down and in need of a glass of wine and a chat. They did their work, occasionally had a coffee and a panini together at lunchtime, then went home to their own lives. Which in Tess's case had been a curry, a glass of wine and a box set of Game of Thrones. With chocolate. She felt she knew Berry, Luke and Elspeth more after a short time than she ever had with the people she had worked with for over eight years.

'Good heavens!' came a voice behind her with unaccustomed respect, 'That is wonderful. You've caught those – ahem – purple lights perfectly without being too obviously purple fairies with acorn hats on.'

'That's what I was aiming for Elspeth.'

'That's my girl' she smiled, squeezing Tess's shoulder and Tess, who had spent most of her life without a mother's presence, had started to feel a much deeper connection between herself and Elspeth, and knew that her aunt felt it too.

'This is perfect for creating your artwork' Elspeth looked up through the glass roof, 'The light falls just right. I hope you're going to continue to use it and not finish when these canvases are done?'

'Now I've got back into it, I really don't want to give up. Could I possibly put the odd, relevant painting up for sale at the museum?' she asked, hesitantly.'

'You can and Sally was asking a couple of months ago for any suggestions for her tea rooms. The walls are bare apart from the odd decorative plate on display, so she'd be happy to have free internal décor in return for them having a price tag on. They would have to be smaller than these of course. I'll have a word with her.'

*

The work on the museum went on as Weaver's Green basked in a long hot summer. Windows were widened or added, making the inside much lighter. The display cases became more viewer-friendly and included some interactive activities. Rather than being shoved back at the sides, the displays now made you meander round and consequently made the space feel much bigger. Quiz sheets regarding the displays were being printed up for the children to answer and get a free witchy bookmark as a prize.

Just behind the reception desk was the area set aside for storytelling, craft displays and occasional living history people in costume, who would answer questions. For the first craft session, Elspeth had booked a friend of hers well in advance, to show how to make corn dollies, especially the traditional Yorkshire spiral or drop dolly.

Elspeth had her witch's costume ready and a humorous story about an incompetent witch from the village of Hawkshurst. She had explained to Tess that although children loved scary things, it was only within reason and could easily tip over into the child wanting to make a swift exit from the museum. A little humour took the edge off. Everything in the museum, even Elspeth, had to be child-friendly.

A new display case housed Elspeth's and other folklore books of the district. When Tess had finished the large canvases, they and other illustrations yet to come, would be used in a new hardback and pleasingly aesthetic version of Elspeth's 'Folklore, myths and legends of the North Yorkshire Moors.'

The 'Conservatory Coffee Café' as Tess and Elspeth had taken to calling it in the absence of a proper name, was the last thing to be finished. Kevin had only been able to work an odd day or two as he had been working on doing up the Hall so he and his family could pack up their old life in Wakefield and move into Rook Hall. Elspeth had told them they could move in anytime as far as she was concerned. The sooner the better. So they had taken her at her word and as of yesterday, they were now the newest residents of the village.

Elspeth had told everyone involved with the museum restoration, including the allotment society from the field behind who had helped whenever they could, that there would be a private viewing when it was well on the way to being finished and before it was officially open to the public.

Earlier, as the day of this private viewing dawned, Tess helped Brian carry the canvases over to the museum. Tess would then decide on the best height to hang them on the bare white walls and Brian would do the honours, with Kevin on stand-by to lift them up to him.

There was still a lot of finishing off to do, not least with the conservatory which would have to be off-limits behind a large sheet of polythene. Nevertheless, it all looked very presentable.

Elspeth was now bouncing about like a two-year-old at the Grange. Tess was glad that her aunt was so happy about her pet project but her enthusiasm was starting to make Tess feel giddy.

'Oh, the bottles' shouted Elspeth, running past Tess in the hallway.

'I've got them' Tess shouted after her.

'Oh, my speech!' Elspeth ran past her again to the study, executing a speedy ninety-degree turn.

Speech? thought Tess and then she had to jump back to avoid getting flattened as Elspeth flew out of the study, then back in again.

'I remember where I put it now' she squawked.

'Take the ring off, Elspeth.'

'What did you say?' Elspeth stopped in her tracks.

'I said take the ring off. It's making you manic. You' - and me, thought Tess – 'need a rest from it.'

Elspeth looked down at the Balefire ring with puzzlement on her face, then took it off. Immediately she did so, she took a step back and collapsed into her chair with her head back, her mouth open and her eyes closed.

Tess waited a minute.

'I'm not fooled for a minute, you old fraud.' said Tess.

The fraud opened one eye and grinned.

'Well honestly. It's not going to make much difference in my disposition now. The ring is back in my possession where it belongs. It's home.'

She put the ring back on, accepted Tess's hand to pull her up and together they set off for the museum.

Luke had been put in charge on the door and was now handing out glasses of sparkling wine as they arrived. Tess put the bottles of sparkling elderflower presse down for the non-drinkers. Olive and Gwen came over as Luke held one of the bottles up and he poured their elderflower. He gave Tess a glass of wine and as he did so, leant forward and whispered in her ear.

'Tess, you are so talented, you've been hiding your light under a bushel. The paintings are wonderful, well done' and he kissed her ear softly which sent shivers through her which took her by surprise.

'Thank you' she said inadequately and shyly, like a schoolgirl.

Somebody clapped their hands together in the communal space in the middle of the floor and everyone stopped talking immediately. Elspeth, of course. She could even command silence from a troop of chattering chimps. They moved towards her like moths to a flame.

'Dearly Beloved. We are gathered here today-' she began, as people started laughing. There was no sign of her written speech. 'I just wanted to say a few words. The people Tess and I have invited here specially today have been instrumental in helping me realise my dream of getting the new Folklore Museum of Weaver's Green up and running again. You have not only done the physical labour, be it getting brochures printed up and organising displays and models, to building, plastering and painting and even keeping us supplied with tea, biscuits and encouragement. You have also put your heart into it and in doing so, have brought us all together again as we used to be. This wouldn't have happened without you all pulling together and I can't tell you how much we appreciate it. I hope the venture will be successful…'

'I don't see why not' interrupted Gwen in peril of receiving a 'look' but got away with it because she was Gwen, 'It was always busy even before you shut it down and it's much better now. Visitors to the village are always asking when you're going to start it up again.'

'It's fondly remembered by people in Whitby too. It has been sorely missed' added Luke, putting his hand to his heart theatrically and heaving a sigh.

Elspeth laughed.

'Thank you, both of you – and with the vision of my lovely niece Tess and my own, renewed enthusiasm, we will make sure that we and future generations can enjoy the myths and legends that are ingrained in the very structure of this village. They have grown up around here, with our village as the central point and as such are part of every one of us.

Can I just thank my niece, Tess? You have all commented most favourably on the folktale illustrations on the walls, which show not only her incredible artistic talent but also capture the essence of the magic we feel all around us. We may not wholly believe the tales passed down to us by our ancestors as these were different times where the only entertainment was by word of mouth and if the stories were embellished a little for the sake of a better story, then we can presume that they had a basis in fact. We feel our ancestor's presence through these tales. Just to know that the same tales we tell today were told – probably round a fire on the green as we have done – makes our community special. There is a continuity here that, in today's fractured world, is more important than I can possibly say.

The paintings are not the only thing I have to thank Tess for. She has given me hope and brought me back to life when I thought life had no meaning any more. I know I won't be the only one who is happy she will now be running the museum with me and making her life in Weaver's Green – with us.'

Even before the applause started and the cheers rang through the barn, Tess could feel the tears flowing down her cheeks. She could feel Luke put his arm around her and squeeze her shoulder, then she ran across to Elspeth and hugged her tightly. Unbelievably, when she looked up, tears were in Elspeth's eyes too.

Wykeham eyes stared into Wykeham eyes then Elspeth whispered,

'You changed my life even before I got the Balefire ring back. Thank you, Tess.'

Chapter 29

On the day before Apple Day, the heavens opened. To the villagers used to the constant, sunny, warm days they had enjoyed for a while, it was a welcome reprieve from the heat. The gardeners and allotment holders all exchanged the great British standard phrase of 'Well, the gardens needed this rain.' Tally couldn't be dragged out in this weather and had stayed at home with Shep, and was no doubt chasing the mop round the kitchen again as though it were a new breed of dog to play with.

Yet as the rain at one point became torrential, everyone dared to think aloud. Would the weather be like this for the festival? Would all their careful plans be ruined? Tess was thinking the same thing but whenever these doubts were voiced to Elspeth, her stock reply was that it would be fine. People actually seemed satisfied with this, thought Tess. As though Elspeth could control the weather. Although maybe she had envisaged the day, 'seen' it, she thought, then gave her a head a little shake. What will be, will be – as Doris Day once said.

As final details were being processed in England's smallest village hall, Tess knew that they would only be able to get a handful of people in here if rain stopped play tomorrow. The trestle tables currently stacked against one wall took up a good percentage of the floor space.

'So we need as many people as we can get out there on the green at seven-thirty a.m. The festival doesn't start till ten but it all needs setting up before people start to arrive. We've got these volunteers …' and Tess read out a list of names, most of whom were crowded into the hall.

'If you know anyone else who can help, please drag them with you in the morning.'

Des put his hand up.

'The craft ciders are arriving later today and I'm keeping them cool in the fridge until just before 10, in case you think our table is bare and we haven't turned up.'

'Excellent idea Des – and the same with the cakes Sally? I hope your spiced toffee and apple cake is on the menu?'

'It certainly is and yes, I'll be keeping them back until the last minute so they don't melt. Or get waterlogged.' Sally added, pulling a face.

'Keep your faith' said Elspeth calmly. 'Today is our dress rehearsal which means tomorrow will run smoothly.'

'We have people coming in this year from Whitby allotments to sell their produce as we haven't actually produced anything yet' Berry piped up, 'but next year, the honours will be ours!' A cheer went up from the other allotment owners.

'And we have apple seedlings to sell in pots' added George, 'and surplus apples to sell too. There are different varieties that everyone has brought in. The windfalls that haven't gone to make pies and chutneys on Gwen and Olive's stall, will be put in a box for people to help themselves.'

'We have apple-tasting – vote for your favourite apple. We are slicing them obviously so they go round. We are also doing the apple-bobbing for the kiddies' said Shah.

'What about the adults? We like apple bobbing too' said Luke as everyone laughed and agreed.

'Okay' grinned Shah 'and for the alleged adults too then.'

'As soon as this rain stops, which I hope is before tonight,' said Tess 'I need the volunteers, plus ladders, to string the lights up in the trees near the storytelling area. They need to charge in the - we hope - sunshine tomorrow so they will twinkle like stars and enhance Elspeth's storytelling.'

'We'll get it done, don't worry. Are the lights here?' said Luke.

'No they're still in a box at the Grange, I'll bring them down later.'

'We *are* dancing twice tomorrow, aren't we? Timed so we don't clash with the folk band?' asked Steven as Tess confirmed they were. She was still in shock at finding out that dour-faced Steven was a closet Morris Dancer. It was strange learning of the hidden depths people had.

'And Herne's Hunters will be performing for an hour in the afternoon and again throughout the evening' said Des. 'When is the stage being set up?'

The stage was, in fact, the village hall dais which was made up of ten, two-foot square blocks, fifteen inches high – but would at least elevate the band a little.

'That's scheduled for first thing, before the tables' said Tess 'because they want it all set up for a sound check at nine-fifteen.'

Tess and Grainne, the local headteacher, were running a 'Throw apples at your teacher' event. The other two teachers were going to sit with their feet in the village stocks at the other side of the green and the apples would be apple-shaped sponges soaked in a bucket of water. Grainne had said the children would love this and enter into it a little too enthusiastically as, however much they liked their teachers, the sight of them soaking wet and helpless against the onslaught would be the highlight of their year.

Suddenly, the relentless drumming of the rain on the roof and against the windows subsided. They had all been shouting to each other against the noise but it now felt like they had to whisper into the silence that had been created. A voice spoke softly in Tess's ear.

'Shall we go and fetch those lights now; in case it starts again?'

'It won't' she said, as sure now as Elspeth had been, 'but we might as well. I think we're more or less finished here and everyone here seems to know what they're doing.'

Catching Elspeth's eye, Tess pointed to the door and got a nod in reply as she and Luke slipped out into the rain-soaked village street.

Not only had the rain stopped but the sun was shining brightly again as if on duty to dry it all up as quickly as possible. Only the sound of the occasional lingering raindrops dripping from the trees could be heard in an otherwise silent village. Whatever residents weren't crammed into the village hall like sardines, were still in their houses, not sure yet if it was safe to come out.

Yet as Tess looked up into a clear blue sky, she was sure now that the rain was gone and would remain so until Apple Day was over. They had almost reached the Grange when Luke grabbed her hand.

'Come on' he said and pulled her on the road to the moors behind the Grange. 'Do you remember after the night you found Tally and I said how wonderful the countryside was after that almighty storm?'

'When I called you poetic as you waxed lyrical about it and you wrote me that absurd…'

'…masterpiece?' Luke threw in.

'Masterpiece, of course' smiled Tess.

'Now you can see what I meant.' Luke indicated with his arm the vast expanse of the moors before them and then turned back towards the valley. The grass *did* seem greener than before. The pockets of trees on the edge of the moor moved with a new and vigorous energy and the heather… Tess realised she had only seen the start of the season when she arrived but now, seeing it in all its purple, glistening splendour in the aftermath of the rain, she knew it was showing its full beauty now.

'Can you smell it too?' whispered Luke as though they were in a cathedral, 'that certain smell after rainstorms as the roads begin to dry and the earth takes the moisture down for its refreshment? The smell of sun after rain always reminds me of Weaver's Green'. He turned towards the village, as did Tess.

It nestled in the valley, as it had done for times long past. The houses, the church, the green, were all brought into sharp definition after the rain. All these separate parts, as Tess watched, seemed to become one complete and radiant whole. Weaver's Green.

'I've come home' whispered Tess to herself.

*

Later at the Grange, after a long day and in anticipation of another, longer one the next day, they prepared for an early night. Tess wondered aloud.

'Why am I a d'Evreux and not a Wykeham d'Evreux? I mean, I know Dad and Francis are just d'Evreux but they're males. Aren't the females supposed to have the Wykeham name attached too, as you have?'

Elspeth looked up, interested in this train of thought.

'The Wykeham name, although just meant to pass down the female line, has always been passed down from mother to daughter, which in the past, there has been a plentiful supply of' she explained. 'As you know, I've let the side down by not having a daughter of my own.' She let the point linger as Tess looked thoughtful.

'Although' Elspeth finally continued, 'You are my grand-niece and the nearest female that I could pass it on to. It doesn't have to be a daughter, just a true Wykeham to continue the name.' She looked up at Tess, 'And you are the daughter I never had.'

Tess met her eyes and they exchanged meaningful smiles.

'Would it be alright with you then, if I used the name Wykeham too?' she asked hesitantly.

'I would consider it a great honour if you did. You are a true Wykeham you know. I wasn't sure at first but now it's beyond doubt.' Elspeth squeezed her arm fondly.

I actually *feel* like a real Wykeham which is why I would like to carry the name. Your name.'

'We can do it through the solicitor? I'll get on to him' said Elspeth, eagerly.

'Thank you, I'd like that Elspeth.'

'You'd better tell your father first, although from what he said to me when he came up here, I think he may be expecting it.'

253

'Although, if I ever *do* get married' her mind already on a different train of thought, 'I might have to drop the d'Evreux.'

'I'm sure it will come as no hardship to you as you've never been completely at ease with it, have you? I'm sure the Conqueror will forgive you, especially as there is Francis to carry that name on.' Elspeth paused, lost in thought, then went on, 'Mm, Theresa Wykeham d'Evreux Mills. Quite a mouthful, I suppose.'

'Elspeth...' warned Tess.

'Or any other surname. I just picked that one at random' she said, airily and unconvincingly. 'If you *did* want to carry the name on however, you could always call your first son Devreux?'

'In your dreams!' shot back Tess.

Chapter 30
APPLE DAY

The Apple Day festival started early with a spectacular sunrise, covering the village of Weaver's Green and the surrounding moors in a soft, warm light and promising much for the rest of the day.

Everyone had turned up bright and early, drawn out of their beds by the fingers of sunshine beckoning through their windows. As they were setting up their tables on the green, Tess looked up at the cloudless, azure sky which heralded a perfect day. Nature was definitely on their side.

Herne's Hunters were already tuning up on the makeshift stage. There were muted guitar riffs, a rumble of drums and a spirited rendition of 'All Around My Hat', in which the early-rising residents joined in with gusto.

Tess was feeling a little delicate this morning and each drumbeat made her eyes jump. The hard work involved in setting up though, plus iced bottles of water, was bringing her back to normal.

After their post-rainstorm enjoyment of the countryside, Luke and a few of the others had helped her drape the lights through some of the trees and they had all ended up in the Wykeham Arms. Berry and Des, who were already looking like an established couple, joined them whilst Shelley held the fort for half an hour. Life was finally starting to feel good for Tess and she embraced the camaraderie of the company she found herself in.

When everything was set up, they all went off early to their stations by their allotted stalls and waited for the hordes to arrive. They didn't have to wait long when the first people arrived way ahead of time, mostly people from the village who had been milling about for the last twenty minutes. Cars had passed by and been directed to parking spaces. The village hall and museum car parks were pressed into service as well as the school playground and Rook Hall had opened the extensive frontage for visitor's cars too. The rest just pulled in where they could, eventually parking off the moorland roads when numbers increased. Something to plan better for next year, thought Tess as it was obviously going to be popular.

Tess watched as Steven and the other Morris dancers cavorted around the green in flower-laden straw hats and white shirt and breeches. Bells fastened under their knees were jangling with every movement, while they waved white handkerchiefs around. She would never look at Steven in the same way again. They were all being led enthusiastically by a man wearing a horse's head, who roused the audience to join in with the clapping and cheering.

Luke and Danny were doing impromptu demonstrations of apple juggling in between helping sell apple tarts and jars of chutney on Gwen and Olive's stall, along with thirst-quenching apple juice. Tess thought that she had better not go near any apples for a month after this or she might find herself turning into one. Apple overload! Everybody was joining in with the spirit of the day though. It was debatable who was having the most fun with the apple-bobbing, children or adults. The shrieks of laughter came from both.

George was in deep discussion with other gardeners about the comparative qualities of different types of apples and Elspeth was wandering round, showing people what happened when you cut an apple crossways and not top to bottom. People were fascinated to see the centre formed a perfect pentacle – a five-pointed star-which had religious connotations as well as Pagan and was used as a protection from evil spirits.

Over lunchtime, the teachers had a reprieve from the stocks and the water-laden apple-shaped sponges and went off to dry out and have some sustenance for another bout later on. Meanwhile, Luke and Grainne were persuaded to take their places, so as not to disappoint all the children lining up in expectation. The head teacher and the policeman whom they all knew, not only from the village but from giving talks on safety at the school, were welcomed with zealous delight as their new targets. Lucien and Branwen, the school's newest recruits from Rook Hall, were enjoying it as much as the rest and had obviously had no problem making friends with the other children.

As Tess watched Luke laughing as the sponges hit him square on she felt a sudden pull toward him, a flickering feeling in her stomach. She looked away without analysing it and thought instead about Elspeth being asked to be a target in the stocks. She had refused, unsurprisingly as she confessed to Tess it would have been a step too far in the rehabilitation of Miss Wykeham d'Evreux.

'I have to retain *some* dignity' she said to Tess, her nose snootily in the air but her smile belying it.

Fifteen minutes later, after some apple juice and a cheese sandwich (no apple inside, Tess checked) she made her way back to the stocks. Incredibly, she saw Elspeth on her way back from there and couldn't believe the evidence of her eyes. Her aunt's customary 'cottage loaf' bun was flat on her head with unclaimed strands of hair dripping down her animated face. She was also beaming from ear to ear.

'Elspeth! I thought you didn't want to lose your dignity' exclaimed Tess.

'I just didn't want my grand-niece to see me soaking wet. One has to maintain standards in front of family and uphold the great family names.'

Tess surveyed the sodden sight in front of her.

'I can see you now, Elspeth' she said, raising both eyebrows.

'Just pretend you can't' Elspeth replied and squelched off in the direction of home to change her clothes – no doubt in an effort to pretend she wasn't as much fun as she really was. Tally trotted happily next to her with wet whiskers, tummy and paws after apparently investigating the sponge bucket too thoroughly. Luke was making hand signals at her, pointing at Elspeth, then at himself, then making throwing motions, which Tess translated as Luke being Luke in helping to soak her aunt.

A little later, members of the band were wandering separately around the green, one with a guitar and the other with a violin, serenading the festival-goers. Tess was watching Luke joining in with them to serenade the elderly ladies. His blond hair was easy to pick out in the crowd, his happy, handsome face alight with laughter.

He looked up at her and their eyes met for just a second. Tess stopped moving. Stopped thinking. Almost stopped breathing. The sounds of the celebrations faded into the background. Her eyes saw nothing but the future and the future was with this man. She saw nothing else but it was enough. Her eyes started focussing again and she looked around, slowly coming to her senses.

As she did so, she caught the eye of her aunt, now dressed up as a witch. Elspeth stared at Tess, their eyes meeting again in silent communication. Tess nodded to her as Elspeth, satisfied, smiled and nodded back. Perhaps then, it was useless to fight her destiny?

There was a lovely surprise as her father appeared early in the afternoon.

'Dad! What are you doing here? It's great to see you.'

'You mentioned it in the last few emails and I was intrigued, then Elspeth, who I have also been exchanging emails with asked if I was coming over. I thought it was a good idea and I'm sure I'll be a more frequent visitor over here to see my lovely daughter and my new, improved aunt' he said with a wink.

The next minute he had been cornered by the vicar of St. Peter's and they were heard discussing the role of ancient monuments in relation to the origins of church sites.

Then as the day went on, the numbers decreased but everyone had congregated around the stage. The last of the afternoon's strong sun started to weaken to a more tolerable level and everyone that Tess talked to seemed very relaxed and happy. Everyone to a man, woman and child, expressed a hope it would be back next year and that they would see her for the Halloween celebrations.

Herne's Hunters had started with a rousing set of folk songs, guaranteed to get everyone singing and dancing, including the one song that everyone knows, The Wild Rover, inducing much foot stomping. As the evening went on, the softer ballads were sung.

Luke came up and handed her a cold cider He put his arm around her, almost proclaiming his thoughts to the whole village. Tess stiffened, then relaxed in to him, putting her head against his shoulder. This was a new Tess, finding her way and following her instincts, leaving the uptight accountant where she belonged – in the past.

Dusk was starting to fall now. The band were playing As I Walked Through the Meadows. Luke suddenly took her glass and put it with his on the ground. Then he took her hand and gently sang the words of the song to her.

'Then I took this fair maid by the lily-white hand.

On the green mossy bank we sat down,

And I placed a kiss on her sweet rosy lips…'
Then he pulled her to him, kissing her deep and long as she melted in the warmth of his arms. She knew now that she had wanted this for a long time.

'I have loved you since we first met, Tess. I fought it, as I think you have but perhaps now, we can stop fighting and face the future together?'

'Oh, I think so Luke, that sounds perfect to me.'

At that moment, the balefire was lit.

It flickered slowly at first, building up to an orange and yellow flame and sending off that particular scent of apple tree branches into the air, enveloping the people standing around. Then the flames changed to a ruby red. The colour of the Balefire ring.

It was soon blazing in the dug-out firepit in the middle of the green. As if they had been co-ordinated, the fairy lights in the trees flickered into life. The children - and their parents pointed and exclaimed at them as they made their way to sit around the fire. They really did add to the fairy tale atmosphere as Tess had hoped they would.

She stood, Luke next to her holding her hand as Berry, doing the same with Des, looked across and winked. Tess grinned back. Tally had attached herself to Eustace and now sat bolt upright, looking at Elspeth, between him and Sally. All her friends were here. All the people she had met only a couple of months ago and now meant so much to her. They all found a place to sit further out while Elspeth circled the fire.

Elspeth held up her hands and everyone fell silent. The firelight lit her face and showed an ancient beauty in the bones there. She didn't seem of this time. She looked as though she had occupied this place for centuries. Then she began.

Her voice, mesmerising, drew all the listeners in. They couldn't pull their eyes away from her. Her voice held them, enchanted them, as her ancestors' voices had through the ages. They could have been the same audience, with the same hopes and dreams, that were round this fire at any point in the history of the village. The fire cast its light, the tale unfolded – and they listened.

Thank you for reading this book and I do hope you enjoyed it. If you would like to read one or two of Elspeth's stories, then carry on...

Folklore, Myths and Legends of the North Yorkshire Moors.

by Elspeth Wykeham d'Evreux.

The Weaver's Tale

This is a story I heard on my mother's knee, as she heard it from her mother and so on, going back into the mists of time. It is the story of this village and how it came to be known as Weaver's Green. Let me tell it to you as I first heard it.

A long time ago, when giants roamed over these lands and the Fae still lived in the trees, there lived a poor man who had no dwelling. All he owned was a red stone his mother had given to him as she lay dying, telling him to guard it with his life. It was all he had left to remind him of her and, obeying her last wishes, he knew he would never sell it.

The man, who was called the Weaver, travelled the country, staying where he was welcome. The people in the settlements, the farmsteads and the villages looked forward to him coming. For the Weaver didn't weave cloth, he spun stories.

There were shouts of delight as he appeared over the hills and fields and the children ran to greet him, begging him to tell them a tale.

'Not until tonight, around the fire. Then I will tell you your stories' answered the man.

The balefire was lit and very soon, as word had gone out to neighbouring steadings, everyone was gathered round the fire. Their faces made translucent by the firelight, they listened spellbound as the Weaver told his tales.

He had no money but his tales brought him food from the people and a bed for the night. Sometimes, they would offer him a pair of shoes or an item of clothing too if he would tell his stories at marriages or handfastings. Sometimes he would be called upon to tell stories at a wake to send the body on its journey.

One day he passed by a tower. He didn't knock to ask if the owner would like to hear a story because he knew an ogre lived there. He was eight feet tall with warts covering his skin and he was cursed with a terrible temper.

This time though, the enormous wooden door opened and the ogre shouted to him, so that all the trees around shook from their roots.

He had heard that the Weaver told tales that could make anyone curl up with laughter. The ogre said that he would wager a pot of gold against the Weaver's life, that he couldn't make him laugh, as he hadn't laughed in two hundred years.

It just so happened that the Weaver had one such tale that he dare not tell, as it was so funny that people who heard it had died laughing. He knew he would be killed anyway if he refused, so he took up the challenge and went inside.

Once in the tower he saw, up in a dark corner, a cage hanging there. Inside was a young woman with long dark hair and brilliant blue eyes. The Weaver had never seen eyes as beautiful as hers. She was terrified and whispered down to the Weaver.

'Please help me.'

Straight away, the Weaver told the Ogre he could have his story but not for any pot of gold. If he made the ogre laugh, all he wanted was freedom for himself and the woman. He whispered back to the woman and asked that she kept her ears covered so she couldn't hear the story.

The ogre readily agreed as this way, he would keep his gold and be able to feast on the woman *and* the Weaver.

The Weaver began his tale. He started slowly and seriously and then began to build it up with more humour. Eventually, as the tale became funnier and funnier, the ogre's face changed. It found expressions he hadn't used before which came perilously close to a smile.

As the Weaver reached the end of his story, the ogre's face started to turn red with the effort of not laughing. When the Weaver spoke the last two sentences, there was a roar as loud as a hundred bears and the ogre threw his head back and laughed. He laughed long and loud, he slapped his hands on the table, stamped his feet on the floor and laughed until tears ran down his cheeks.

Suddenly, in the middle of the loudest laugh of all, he fell over backwards, stone dead.

Quickly, the Weaver climbed up and freed the young woman from the cage and together they ran outside to freedom. He didn't take any gold, as ogre's gold was unlucky. Besides, he had all he wanted from life and if he didn't have riches, he had contentment. He told the woman that at least the ogre had died happy and she laughed and kissed his cheek softly.

The Weaver returned the woman to her father who lived, with two of his daughters, in a lush green valley hidden from sight in the middle of the moors. Her father was so pleased that he offered him his daughter Avery, for that was her name, in marriage. The Weaver was delighted as they had both fallen in love on the journey home.

He had his precious red stone set into a ring of her own mother's, uniting the families and gave it to Avery for her betrothal ring.

The Weaver settled there in that fertile valley and their family grew. Eventually, others came to join them and a village grew up around them. Their family lived happily there for hundreds of years and continue to live there now as it still exists today. It is called Weaver's Green, in honour of the brave storyteller.

The Wykeham Witches

In a deep, green valley, hidden amongst heath and heather, dwelt a farmer and his three daughters on a farm named Wykeham Stead.

There, they made a living from the land. Crops grew in the fertile soil and animals grazed on the fresh green grass.

They had been forced to move there from a township further to the north of the land because of the farmer's wife. Her unusual gifts, although used for the good of the people around them, were viewed with suspicion by some.

After his wife, Elburga, had been stoned in the town square, he brought her to this place, where they had found peace. Later, when his wife died, he brought up his three daughters on the land they had settled on. They had inherited their mother's gifts and, although their father cautioned them, they wanted to use these gifts to help people nearby and in the villages some miles distant.

They drove away disease with herbs, delivered babies and even cured lame horses and sheep. Ardith, Denegith and Avery loved humankind and every living creature. They were born healers and used the kitchen garden to grow their medicines.

The Wykeham girls were celebrated for their gifts and people came from miles around for their help. They had other gifts, which because of their father's warning, they tried to suppress, only telling each other and their father of their strange dreams.

One stormy night, Denegith had a waking vision, in which she saw a horse pulling a cart behind it, laden not only with parcels of wool but also a man and woman and their two children. She saw the bridge collapse with the flooded river, carrying the cart and all the people on it, downstream to drown.

She recognised the bridge, it was at a place some distance away and was an old packhorse bridge, which was already in bad repair.

With no hesitation, she saddled up their best horse and rode off into the storm, with her father's words of warning ringing in her ears. She rode through terrible, lashing rain and wind, with lightning hitting the ground all around her. She reached the bridge just before they did and stopped them by blocking their way.

The man, who was a rich wool merchant, didn't believe her story and thought she was a madwoman. He tried to make her move - but the next minute, in front of their eyes, the bridge collapsed, stone on top of stone and crumbled into the raging torrent below. They were so grateful that they offered her money and jewels which she refused, saying she had no need of them, before she rode back home again.

The family went round the way she had told them and eventually reached the nearest town. Next morning they asked around the town, telling everyone of the girl who had saved them. They learnt about the Wykeham girls and so the very next day, three cows, three horses and a crateful of hens arrived at their farm to say thank you for the unselfish act.

Unfortunately, this story was heard by Cyne, the daughter of the local blacksmith. She loved a woodcutter but knew he had loved Denegith since they were children and so didn't even notice her. She took her chance and went to the King's Sheriff, accusing all three Wykeham girls of being witches and causing the bridge to collapse, along with other false accusations.

Denegith and her sisters were brought before the inquisitor and accused of communing with devils and doing unnatural acts for the harm of persons unknown, even to causing death. The people were afraid of witches and the mere word made them act in fear. Denegith said that her sisters had nothing to do with the accident and were innocent and as this could be proved by the merchant's story, they were allowed to go.

The Town Guild decreed that nobody was allowed to speak for her and she was condemned to be whipped in the streets until she was dead. Her sisters wept as they walked alongside her on her last journey. Eventually, her strength gone, Denegith brought her eyes up to meet those of her accuser, Cyne's. With her last, dying breath, she spoke a curse.

'You will reap the consequence of your wicked accusation. You will die without issue and live without love.'

The remaining Wykeham girls lived quietly with their father, eventually marrying and living there with their families. They kept out of harm's way, only helping their friends whom they could trust. If they had any more visions, they kept it to themselves.

The daughters came to be known as the Wykeham Witches but were revered as a force for good because of all the help they gave to other people. They were not associated with evil and lived out their lives in peace.

Their descendants, even now, live in the same area and still carry the same distinguished blood.

The Gytrash of Godesmere

Around the forests, moors, heaths and wastelands of this country, there have always been stories of Black Dogs. The moors of North Yorkshire have their own Black Dog – The Gytrash of Godesmere.

This awful apparition has blood-red eyes, huge dripping fangs and long, sharp claws.

The Gytrash was first seen on the roads leading to Godesmere village, where it roamed alongside, waiting for any unsuspecting travellers. Sometimes these travellers saw horses or crows but nearly all the reports were about a huge black dog – from those who survived!

It led the unlucky travellers astray into the bogs and mires far away from the road, where they would wander around, lost for all eternity. Sometimes there were reports that, occasionally benevolent, they would lead a lost traveller onto the right road.

The Gytrash also could be heard howling over the moors, especially when the moon was full. It often indicated a local death in a nearby house. Sometimes, the black dog's appearance merely foretold a time of chaos to come or even a time of renewal.

The legends of the Gytrash and other black dogs still carry on today. People travelling the moorland roads across the country tell of huge black shapes with red eyes, prowling by the side of the roads.

...and you can be sure that none of them were called Tallulah!

Printed in Great Britain
by Amazon

36476958R00154